simply shellfish

leslie glover pendleton

simply SHELLFISH

quick and easy recipes

for shrimp, crab, scallops,

clams, mussels, oysters, lobster,

squid, and sides

WM WILLIAM MORROW *An Imprint of* HarperCollins*Publishers*

HarperCollins books may be purchased for educational, business, or sales promotional use. For information please write: Special Markets Department, HarperCollins Publishers, 10 East 53rd Street, New York, NY 10022.

FIRST EDITION

Designed by Fritz Metsch

Printed on acid-free paper

Library of Congress Cataloging-in-Publication Data

Pendleton, Leslie Glover.
    Simply shellfish : Quick and easy recipes for shrimp, crab, scallops, clams, mussels, oysters, lobster, squid, and sides / Leslie Glover Pendleton.—1st ed.
        p. cm.
    Includes index.
    ISBN-13: 978-0-06-073500-5
    ISBN-10: 0-06-073500-7
    1. Cookery (Shellfish)   I. Title.

TX753.P46   2006
641.6'94—dc22   2005046101

06 07 08 09 10   WBC/QW   10 9 8 7 6 5 4 3 2 1

for papadede

contents

acknowledgments

As always, there are many people whose generous gifts of time, knowledge, and interest helped give birth to this book. Creating recipes is a process of innovation, experimentation, and inspiration. I especially thank those food writers, chefs, and teachers who have offered me inspiration as well as information: Antonia Allegra, Jean Anderson, Rosemary Barron, Julia Child, Craig Claiborne, Jane Kirby, James Peterson, Peter Reinhart, Leslie Revsin, Waverly Root, Arthur Schwartz, John Shields, Hiroko Shimbo, Nina Simonds, Fred Thompson, Paula Wolfert, and the many members of The Episcopal Church of Our Saviour, Hillandale, Maryland, who joyfully shared their native cooking with me.

Thank you, Honey Konicoff and the people at Phillips Seafood, for sharing their wealth of knowledge and research on the subject of crab; Nicholas Furman and the Oregon Dungeness Crab Commission; Chesapeake Maritime Museum (especially the oystering exhibit); John Anagnos, of City Fish Market in Wethersfield, Connecticut, for letting me pick his brain, which holds a lifetime of seafood retail experience; Bob Bayer at The Lobster Institute in Maine, and Max's Oyster Bar in West Hartford, Connecticut.

Thanks to Lucy Baker, Susan Friedland, and Harriet Bell for a critical eye and belief in the subject, and my agent, Lisa Ekus, for helping me see the obvious. My parents, Tom and Diane Glover, food connoisseurs, critical tasters, and constant support team; the staff at Christ Church Cathedral, Hartford, Connecticut, for being devoted tasters; and of course, my husband, Mark, and children, Will and Lydia, for their support, trying one more oyster, helping to clean up, and offering their culinary opinions.

When I told people the subject of the cookbook I was working on—shellfish—eyes widened, and friends oooh-ed and offered to be my tasters. Shellfish is the cream of the ocean crop. Just the mention of a lobster dinner or grilled shrimp makes us think of luxurious, indulgent special occasions. Best of all, all seafood is incredibly healthy. As we try to incorporate more fish into our everyday diets, it is important not to overlook the vast possibilities in the shellfish category.

There is no need to wait for a celebration to enjoy clams, mussels, oysters, lobster, scallops, shrimp, squid, and crab. They are low in fat and full of protein, minerals, and heart-healthy omega-3 fatty acids. Their varied rich, sweet, briny, nutty flavors lend themselves to simple preparations, and they are the fastest cooking protein around. For an easy weeknight meal there is nothing faster or more satisfying than a bowl of glistening black mussels in a steaming, briny broth with a good bread and green salad on the side.

Shellfish are commonly broken down into several groups: mollusks, gastropods, crustaceans, bivalves, and cephalopods. A mollusk is any marine animal with no vertebrae. A gastropod is a mollusk housed in a single shell, such as a conch or snail. A crustacean is an anthropod with a segmented body, exoskeleton, and paired, jointed limbs. Lobsters, crabs, shrimp, and crawfish are all crustaceans. A bivalve is a mollusk that lives inside two hinged shells. Clams, mussels, oysters, and scallops are all bivalves. Cephalopods, such as squid and octopus, have conical heads, either eight or ten tentacles, and they all produce ink. While they do not technically have a shell, squid are considered shellfish because of their internal quill, which resembles a thin, clear, flexible plastic.

In this book I have dealt with the most common shellfish: shrimp, crab, scallops, clams and mussels, oysters, lobsters, and squid. The techniques are simple, and flavors are borrowed from cuisines around the world. Most of the recipes can be completed in under thirty minutes, and when a recipe can be made completely or partially ahead of time it is clearly noted. Once you are familiar with the basics, they can be applied to any shellfish you come across. If you are lucky enough to find sweet and creamy Long Island bay scallops in their brief summer season, you can treat them like any other kind of scallop and use them in the recipes in this book. Or if cockles are at your local market, try steaming them like larger hard-shelled clams or mussels. Freshwater prawns, langoustines, or any other unusual crustacean can be substituted for shrimp or lobster. Just remember to adjust the cooking time; little clams and scallops take less time to cook than their larger cousins. Each shellfish recipe lists suggestions for side dishes to make a meal, and references those recipes found in the Sides, Vegetables, and Salads chapter.

As always, look for the freshest fish, get to know your fish seller or seafood market manager, and ask questions. Seafood people love to talk seafood, and if they don't, find a new one. But, most important, have fun, experiment, cook with confidence, and eat well!

Crustacean   An anthropod with a segmented body, exoskeleton, and paired, jointed limbs. Lobster, crab, shrimp, crawfish

Cephalopod   Squid is categorized as a shellfish because of its internal quill, which resembles thin, clear, flexible plastic. Often, even in cleaned squid, a piece of the quill is left inside the body sac, and should be pulled out and discarded. This "shell" has no known function. Octopus is also a cephalopod but does not have a shell.

Bivalve   A mollusk that lives inside two hinged shells. Clams, mussels, oysters, scallops

Mollusk   This classification refers to marine animals with no vertebrae. Crustaceans are not classified as mollusks because they have exoskeletons.

Gastropod   A mollusk housed in a single shell, such as a conch or snail.

the flavor in the shell

In today's skinless, boneless convenience food–obsessed world, we have forgotten how much flavor that skin and those bones can impart. When it comes to chicken, I often don't have the time or energy to make stock and will reach for a can. But when making a shellfish soup or bisque there are few substitutes for the rich essence of lobster, crab, or shrimp, which comes from coaxing the amplitude of flavor left behind in their shells. Some stocks are time consuming and better left to restaurant kitchens, where they can roast veal bones and vegetables and simmer them slowly for 8 hours or more. However, shellfish stock is easy and quick. Simmer lobster, shrimp, or crab shells for 30 minutes and you have the base for another fabulous meal. Use the stock right away or freeze for another time.

The shells from 2 to 4 pounds
of lobster, shrimp, or crab
(cooked or raw)
3 tablespoons olive or
vegetable oil
1 bay leaf
2 celery ribs, coarsely
chopped
1 carrot, coarsely chopped
1 onion, quartered

lobster, shrimp, or crab shell stock

If the shellfish has been boiled, save the cooking water and use it in place of the water called for in the recipe.

1. Chop or break the shells into small pieces. In a large pot, cook the shells in the oil over moderate heat, stirring, for 10 minutes. Add the remaining ingredients and cover with cold water (or cooking liquid). Bring the water to a boil and simmer, uncovered, for 30 minutes.

2. Strain the stock through a fine sieve, discard the solids, and return the stock to the pot. Simmer until it is reduced to 3 cups and let cool.

The stock can be refrigerated for up to 48 hours or frozen for up to 6 months.

shrimp

with rock shrimp and crawfish

It is difficult to know what kind of shrimp you are buying and where they are from, since there are so many types of shrimp and so many countries that harvest them. Three-quarters of the shrimp consumed in the United States is imported and most of that is farm raised. Shrimp are rarely available fresh (meaning never been frozen) because shrimpers usually behead and freeze them while at sea. In fact, I recommend buying shrimp frozen so that you can have control over thawing them rather than the supermarket or fish store. If you do not see frozen shrimp displayed, just ask. There are usually more in the back.

purchasing

Individually frozen shrimp should not have large amounts of frost around them or dry-looking white spots. This implies thawing and refreezing, and freezer burn. Shrimp frozen in blocks of ice are usually immune to this problem, but they are not as convenient to use.

If there is a sale on thawed shrimp in a display case, ask if you can buy them still frozen. Thawed shrimp should look firm and intact, without any dark spots. Use thawed shrimp within 48 hours.

sizes

The only real standard for shrimp size is count per pound. Any reference to medium, large, jumbo, etc., is purely subjective. One store's large is another store's jumbo and the larger the shrimp, the higher the price. I do not specify sizes in recipes where it does not matter.

to devein or not to devein?

Sometimes I do, sometimes I don't. Sorry to be so vague, but it depends on the shrimp. I have had farm-raised shrimp so clean I can't even find the digestive tract on the rounded side. Others are big and gritty (though this is rarely the case). Make a shallow slit down the backs of a few shrimp, remove the vein, and see what you think. Slitting shrimp down the back has other advantages. It is easier to see if the shrimp is cooked through by looking into the cut, it is attractive, and it provides more surface area for sauces and marinades.

rock shrimp and crawfish

In this chapter, shrimp is called for in every recipe; size is specified only when necessary. Peeled rock shrimp can be substituted, as can crayfish in the shell or peeled tails, depending on preference.

rock shrimp

These deepwater shrimp, with rock-hard shells (thus the name), have only recently appeared on the market in significant amounts, since a machine was invented to remove the armorlike shell. Extracting the meat used to be too labor-intensive, so rock shrimp were thrown back when caught. Peeled rock shrimp are small (70 to 90 per pound) and have the similar sweet taste and firm texture of rock lobster. They can be substituted in most shrimp recipes where small shrimp would be suitable, and paired with sauces in shrimp and lobster recipes. Peak season for rock shrimp is late summer and autumn.

crawfish

Crawfish look like miniature lobsters and taste like a cross between lobster and shrimp. Louisiana is the country's crawfish capital, where people prefer to consume them boiled by the pound and messy, accompanied by butter, beer, and music. The prized part of the crawfish, the tail meat, is available peeled and frozen, and can be substituted in most shrimp recipes. Frozen, cooked whole crawfish can be added to a dish at the end of cooking, just to be heated through, but keep in mind that 1 pound of whole crawfish equals 2 to 3 ounces of tail meat.

When eating plain, boiled crawfish, allow 2 to 4 pounds per person. Simmer live crawfish in a pot of salted boiling water for about 10 minutes.

dilled shrimp spread

This multipurpose shrimp spread can be used as a dip with vegetables and crackers, a spread for bagels or tea sandwiches, or a filling for cherry tomatoes or cucumber slices. Try different fresh herbs to create your own variation.

makes about 1 ⅓ cups

½ pound peeled shrimp, rock shrimp, or crawfish tails

2 tablespoons butter

1 garlic clove, chopped

3 ounces cream cheese

⅓ cup chopped celery

1 tablespoon Dijon mustard

1 tablespoon chopped fresh dill

1. In a small skillet, cook the shrimp in the butter over medium-high heat, stirring, for 1 to 3 minutes, or until just cooked through. Transfer the shrimp and juices to a food processor.

2. Add the remaining ingredients and blend to form a coarse paste. (Do not process until smooth.) Transfer the spread to a medium bowl, stir in salt and pepper to taste, and chill, covered, for at least 1 hour.

The spread keeps, covered and refrigerated, for up to 3 days.

pickled shrimp and onions with mexican flavors

The classic Yucatán condiment, pickled red onions, joins with an equally classic favorite of the American South, pickled shrimp, to produce a dish pretty in pink and flecked with green. Serve with the classic southern preference, Ritz crackers, or classic Mexican tortilla chips.

serves 8 as a first course
or as an hors d'oeuvre

1 large red onion, thinly sliced
(about 2 cups)

2 fresh jalapeño or serrano
chiles, sliced very thin
crosswise (including the
seeds)

1½ cups distilled white
vinegar

1 cup orange juice

1½ teaspoons whole cumin
seeds

2 teaspoons salt

2 pounds peeled shrimp

¼ cup chopped fresh cilantro

1. In a large saucepan, combine the onion and enough water to cover. Bring the water to a boil and drain.

2. Return the onion to the saucepan and add ½ cup water and the remaining ingredients except the cilantro. Bring the mixture to a boil and immediately transfer to a heatproof bowl and let cool. Cover and refrigerate the shrimp for at least 2 hours. Garnish with fresh cilantro.

The shrimp keep for up to 3 days.

shrimp with melon and prosciutto

These simple cold hors d'oeuvres are a twist on the classic appetizer of prosciutto and melon. Other fruits such as pear or jicama can be substituted for the melon.

10 large raw shrimp
  (see Note)
20 small slices cantaloupe,
  about 2 X 1 X ¼ inch
3 to 5 thin slices prosciutto,
  halved, cut into strips
  about 1 X 3 inches
½ teaspoon honey
1 tablespoon balsamic
  vinegar
2 tablespoons olive oil
Freshly ground black pepper

1. In a large saucepan, bring 2 inches of water to a boil. Add the shrimp and cook, covered, 1 to 2 minutes, or until just cooked through. Drain, then rinse immediately in cold water to stop the cooking, and chill for 30 minutes until cold. Peel the shrimp.

2. Halve each shrimp lengthwise. Wrap a piece of shrimp and cantaloupe together with a strip of prosciutto and secure with a toothpick. Arrange the hors d'oeuvres on a plate.

3. In a small bowl, dissolve the honey in the vinegar. Add the oil and whisk until emulsified. Drizzle over the hors d'oeuvres and sprinkle with pepper to taste.

Note: Precooked shrimp can be used as a shortcut. Omit step 1.

roasted shrimp on asparagus skewers with brie

Using asparagus to skewer shrimp is a fun way to connect the vegetable and main course. Brie, one of the few kinds of cheese that go well with seafood, adds a bit of creaminess to this simple dish. Serve this already colorful dish with Jollof Rice (page 168), Sprouts and Sliced Tomato Salad (page 179), or Red, White, and Blue Slaw (page 183).

serves 4 as a main course
or 10 as an hors d'oeuvre

1½ pounds raw shrimp, peeled (25 per pound or larger)

¾ to 1 pound asparagus, scrubbed and the tough ends trimmed

1 tablespoon balsamic vinegar

½ teaspoon salt

½ teaspoon black pepper

2 tablespoons olive oil

4 ounces Brie, rind discarded

1. Preheat the oven to 450°F.

2. Butterfly the shrimp by halving them lengthwise through the rounded side without cutting all the way through. In the middle of each shrimp, cut a ½-inch section of the slit all the way through, wide enough for an asparagus spear to pass through. Thread 2 to 3 shrimp onto each asparagus spear, leaving space between them.

3. In a small bowl, whisk together the vinegar, salt, and pepper. Add the oil and whisk until emulsified.

4. Arrange threaded asparagus and leftover asparagus in a single layer in a shallow baking pan or cookie sheet with sides, and brush with the dressing. Roast in the middle of the oven for 10 to 12 minutes, or until the shrimp is just cooked through.

5. Remove from the oven and immediately top each shrimp with some of the Brie. (The Brie will melt from the heat.) Serve 2 to 3 shrimp skewers per person with additional plain asparagus on the side.

Note: To make individual skewers for hors d'oeuvres, cut the asparagus spears between the shrimp after roasting.

almond shrimp with curried mango and sweet potato

A curried mango and sweet potato salad is prepared first, then combined with rich, nutty shrimp, resulting in a unique, delicious dish sure to impress any guest. Underripe or green mangoes have a pleasant tart flavor and crispness that balance well with the soft sweet potato. Serve it with Grapefruit Rice with Chives (page 171) and Sliced Asparagus and Edamame with Olive Oil (page 176).

serves 4

½ cup vegetable or olive oil

1 medium sweet potato,
   peeled and cut into ¼-inch
   dice (about 2 cups)

1 firm, underripe mango,
   peeled and cut into ¼-inch
   dice (about 2 cups)

2 teaspoons curry powder

1½ tablespoons red or white
   wine vinegar

1 tablespoon Dijon mustard

1½ pounds raw large shrimp,
   peeled and deveined

½ cup almonds, finely ground
   in a food processor

½ teaspoon salt

½ teaspoon freshly ground
   black pepper

½ cup coarsely chopped
   fresh cilantro

1. In a large skillet, heat ¼ cup of the oil over moderate heat until hot. Add the sweet potato and sauté, stirring, for 3 minutes. Add the mango and cook, stirring, for 2 minutes. Stir in the curry powder and cook, stirring, for 1 to 2 minutes, or until the sweet potato is just tender. Transfer the mixture to a bowl and stir in ½ cup water, the vinegar, mustard, and salt and pepper to taste. Set aside at room temperature.

The sweet potato–mango mixture can be made up to 8 hours in advance. Serve at room temperature.

2. Wipe out the skillet. In a large bowl, toss together the shrimp, almonds, salt, and pepper. Heat the remaining ¼ cup oil in the skillet over moderately high heat. Add half the shrimp mixture, and sauté the shrimp for 1 to 2 minutes on each side, or until they just curl. With a slotted spoon, transfer them to a plate. Sauté the remaining shrimp in the same manner.

3. Return all the shrimp to the skillet and add the mango mixture. Heat, stirring, just until heated through. Serve immediately, sprinkled with the cilantro.

Note: Some people cannot get enough cilantro, while others find the flavor overwhelming, so I usually serve the cilantro in a separate bowl, for diners to add as desired.

grilled garlic shrimp fajitas

One of my favorite ways to grill shrimp is with a simple garlic butter, whether I'm serving them in tortillas or alone with vegetables. When I do fajitas I set up a table near the grill and let people devour them as they are cooked. Guests love the informal hands-on approach of wrapping golden, succulent shrimp, fresh off the grill, in warm, soft flour tortillas and garnishing them to their taste. Have some Quick Pickled Green Beans (page 178), Jollof Rice (page 168), or Two Potato Hash (page 170) standing by to make it a meal.

makes 8 fajitas; serves 4

1½ pounds large shrimp, peeled and deveined, or peeled rock shrimp or crawfish tails

3 tablespoons butter

2 large garlic cloves

½ cup sour cream

3 tablespoons mayonnaise

3 tablespoons milk

¼ teaspoon ground cumin

Salt

8 small ("fajita size") flour tortillas

2 to 3 cups finely shredded green cabbage

Bottled green tomatillo salsa

1. Thread the shrimp onto metal skewers without crowding them. (Bamboo skewers can be used in place of metal ones, but they must be soaked in warm water for at least 1 hour to keep them from catching fire.)

2. In a small saucepan or microwave, melt the butter and add the garlic, forced though a garlic press or minced to a paste.

3. In a small bowl stir together the sour cream, mayonnaise, milk, and cumin and reserve.

4. Grill the shrimp on a preheated grill, brushing often with the garlic butter, until cooked through, about 4 minutes on each side (less for smaller rock shrimp or crawfish). Season the shrimp lightly with salt. (Alternatively, the shrimp can be broiled in a shallow pan, 6 inches from the heat.)

5. Grill or broil the tortillas for 30 seconds on each side (they may puff up) and transfer to a brown paper bag to keep them warm (see Note).

6. To serve, wrap some of the shrimp in a warm tortilla with the cabbage, sour cream sauce, and green salsa. Eat out of hand.

Note: Transferring the warmed tortillas to a brown paper bag keeps them warm for up to 20 minutes. I like to roll down the top of the bag and put it right on the table, on its side so diners can serve themselves.

shrimp and sausage kebabs

Like ham and bacon, salty and spicy sausage makes a great combination with briny, rich shrimp. Add Potato Salad with Roasted Peppers and Sesame Seeds (page 169), or Two Potato Hash (page 170) and Spinach Salad with Blue Cheese and Plum Dressing (page 186) to make a meal.

serves 6

8 large scallions (a.k.a. green onions)

⅓ cup apricot jam

¼ cup fresh lemon juice

½ cup vegetable oil

2 tablespoons soy sauce

1¼ pounds sweet Italian sausage links

1½ pounds large shrimp, peeled and deveined

12 medium white mushrooms, wiped clean

2 green, red, or yellow bell peppers

1. Trim the white parts of the scallions to 4-inch lengths and reserve 2 cups of the greens, coarsely chopped.

2. In a blender or food processor puree the scallion greens, apricot jam, lemon juice, oil, and soy sauce. Put the sausage and shrimp in two separate sealable bags. In a third bag combine the scallion sections, mushrooms, and bell peppers, and divide the marinade among all the bags. Chill and let marinate for 30 minutes to 1 hour.

3. Keeping the three foods separate, thread them onto metal skewers, without crowding, and season with salt and pepper. Cook on a preheated grill; 5 minutes for the shrimp; 15 to 20 minutes for the sausage; and 10 to 15 minutes for the vegetables.

Note: Grilling the foods separately, rather than mixing them on the skewers, ensures that the cook has control over cooking times.

shrimp in spicy tomato, peanut, and ginger sauce

Peanut butter gives this African-style sauce a somewhat silky texture and a subtle nutty flavor. Normally fresh chiles would be used, but pepper flakes provide an easy substitute for the kick in the sauce. In addition to the essential white rice, a green salad, Quick Pickled Green Beans (page 178), Carrot Ribbons with Lemon and Cumin (page 180), or Sliced Asparagus and Edamame with Olive Oil (page 176) make nice accompaniments.

serves 4

One 14- to 16-ounce
   can tomato puree
   (1¾ to 2 cups)

1 medium onion, chopped
   (about 1½ cups)

2 tablespoons vegetable oil

½ teaspoon hot red pepper
   flakes

2 pounds shrimp (medium to
   large), still in the shells

1 teaspoon ground ginger

2 large garlic cloves, minced

3 tablespoons peanut butter

4 cups cooked white rice as
   an accompaniment

½ cup lightly salted peanuts

1. In a large, deep skillet, simmer the tomato puree, onion, oil, and pepper flakes for 30 minutes, stirring often, until very thick and any excess liquid has evaporated.

2. While the tomato mixture is cooking, peel and devein the shrimp, transferring the shells to a medium saucepan. Add 4 cups water to the shells and simmer for 20 minutes. Strain the broth into a measuring cup. There should be about 2 cups broth. (If there is less, add water to make 2 cups; if there is more, continue to simmer until reduced to 2 cups.)

3. Stir 1 cup of the broth into the tomato sauce with the ginger, garlic, and peanut butter. Simmer, stirring, for 5 minutes.

The sauce can be made up to this point 1 day ahead, covered, and chilled. Reheat before continuing.

4. Add the shrimp and simmer for 10 minutes, or until the shrimp are cooked through. Add additional broth to thin the sauce to the desired consistancy.

5. Serve the shrimp and sauce over rice, sprinkled with the peanuts.

shrimp with escarole and tomatoes

*F*resh, *bright green escarole, simmered with tomatoes and lots of garlic, is one of my favorite Italian side dishes. The addition of shrimp brings it to the center of the plate, making it a hearty and healthy main course, leaving the sides open for* Warm Herbed White Bean Salad *(page 172),* Roasted Maple Butter Acorn Squash *(page 177), or* Orange Orzo with Basil *(page 167).*

serves 4

3 garlic cloves, thinly sliced

¼ cup olive oil

1-pound head of escarole, the
leaves cut in half, washed
well, and spun dry

One 28-ounce can whole
tomatoes, drained

2 pounds peeled shrimp, rock
shrimp, or crawfish tails

1. In a large, deep skillet, cook the garlic in the oil over moderate heat, stirring, until pale golden.

2. Add the escarole and tomatoes, crushing the tomatoes. Simmer the mixture, stirring occasionally, for 3 minutes. Add the shrimp and cook, stirring, about 2 minutes, or until the shrimp are just cooked through.

Note: Escarole is a tough, fibrous, flavorful leafy green (it's actually a type of endive) that can be eaten raw, but holds up well to cooking.

shrimp, feta, and golden onion pizza

Serve this delicious Greek-inspired pizza for dinner with Eggless Caesar Salad (page 188) or cut it into small wedges or squares and serve as an hors d'oeuvre.

serves 2 as a main course
or 6 as an hors d'oeuvre

2 Vidalia onions, thinly sliced

4 tablespoons olive oil

Two 7-inch prebaked pizza
   shells (such as Boboli)

4 ounces feta cheese

1 teaspoon dried oregano

1 large garlic clove, minced

½ pound (1½ cups) small
   frozen cooked shrimp, rock
   shrimp, or crawfish tails,
   thawed

1. Preheat the oven to 500°F.

2. In a large skillet, sauté the onions in 2 tablespoons of the oil over moderately high heat, stirring, until golden, about 15 minutes.

3. Divide the onions between the pizza crusts, spreading evenly. Scatter the feta, oregano, garlic, and shrimp on top. Drizzle each pizza with 1 tablespoon of the remaining oil.

4. Bake the pizzas on a baking sheet in the middle of the oven until the cheese is bubbly and the crust is crisp, 10 to 12 minutes. Serve whole as a main course or cut into squares for hors d'oeuvres.

shrimp with brown butter, pine nuts, and capers

Capers quickly lose their moisture and become crisp when sautéed, and by the time the pine nuts are golden the butter will be brown and aromatic. This quick sauce combined with rich, juicy shrimp is as perfect for a weeknight family meal as it is for an elegant dinner party. Spoon it over cooked rice or egg noodles, or serve it with Baked Vegetable and Cheese Polenta (page 174), Roasted Maple Butter Acorn Squash (page 177), and Eggless Caesar Salad (page 188).

serves 4

½ stick (4 tablespoons) butter

⅓ cup drained capers

⅓ cup pine nuts

1½ pounds medium to large shrimp, peeled and deveined, or peeled rock shrimp or crawfish tails

1 tablespoon fresh lemon juice

1. In a large heavy skillet, heat the butter over moderate heat. Add the capers and cook, stirring, for 3 minutes, or until the butter begins to brown. Add the pine nuts and cook, stirring, for 2 minutes, or until they are golden, being careful not to burn them.

2. Add the shrimp and cook 5 to 8 minutes (1 to 2 minutes for rock shrimp or crawfish), until they curl and are just cooked through. Sprinkle with the lemon juice and serve immediately.

chinese red-cooked shrimp

In her book China Express, *Nina Simonds offers a simplified way to "red cook." Red cooking is a Chinese technique in which food is braised in an anise-spiked, soy sauce–based liquid. By replacing a hard-to-find ingredient, such as star anise, with one that's available in the supermarket, aniseed, and streamlining the technique, this unique dish can be prepared in a snap. Here I've used shrimp, which pick up the flavors quickly without the classic braising time. Suitable side dishes are Grapefruit Rice with Chives (page 171), Sprouts and Sliced Tomato Salad (page 179), or Carrot Ribbons with Lemon and Cumin (page 180).*

serves 4

⅓ cup low-sodium soy sauce

3 tablespoons dry vermouth
   or Scotch

¼ teaspoon aniseed

¼ teaspoon hot red pepper
   flakes

½ cinnamon stick

8 ounces white mushrooms,
   wiped clean and sliced

⅓ cup scallions (a.k.a. green
   onions), coarsely chopped

1½ pounds peeled shrimp,
   rock shrimp, or crawfish
   tails, patted dry

2 tablespoons cornstarch

3 tablespoons vegetable oil

1. In a large saucepan, combine the soy sauce, 1 cup water, the vermouth, aniseed, pepper flakes, and cinnamon stick and simmer for 10 minutes, covered. Strain the sauce through a sieve set over a bowl and return the sauce to the pan. Add the mushrooms and scallions and simmer for 2 minutes.

2. Toss the shrimp with the cornstarch. Heat the oil in a large, heavy skillet over moderately high heat, and fry the shrimp, turning them, for 1 minute. Add the sauce with mushrooms and simmer, uncovered, for 1 minute, or until the shrimp are cooked through. Serve immediately.

Note: Snow peas or broccoli cut into bite-size pieces can be blanched for 1 minute in boiling water, and added to the finished shrimp dish if desired.

shrimp in pepper butter beer sauce

In New Orleans they call it barbecued shrimp. It's not grilled, nor is it sauced in anything that resembles barbecue sauce, but it is spicy and finger-licking good. You've got to have bread to soak up the sauce and a salad on the side to cool the tongue. Other side attractions could be Mom's Coleslaw (page 181), Quick Pickled Green Beans (page 178), or Jollof Rice (page 168).

serves 4

½ cup chopped onions

2 garlic cloves, minced

1 stick (8 tablespoons) butter

½ teaspoon dried thyme

½ teaspoon dried oregano

1 teaspoon freshly ground
   black pepper

½ teaspoon hot red pepper
   flakes

1 teaspoon sweet paprika

1 tablespoon Worcestershire
   sauce

1 cup pale-colored beer

1½ to 2 pounds raw peeled
   shrimp, rock shrimp, or
   crawfish tails

1. In a deep, heavy skillet, cook the onion and garlic in the butter over moderate heat until softened, about 10 minutes.

2. Add the thyme, oregano, black pepper, pepper flakes, and paprika and cook, stirring, for 2 minutes. Increase the heat to moderately high, add the Worcestershire sauce and beer, and boil for 3 minutes.

3. Add the shrimp and cook, stirring, until they are curled and just cooked through. Serve immediately.

shrimp tempura with ginger dipping sauce

Shrimp are coated in a thin batter, which fries to a light and lacy crisp shell. While you're at it, make some extra batter and fry vegetables such as sliced zucchini, eggplant, carrots, broccoli, and snow peas. It is best to eat everything as soon as it is fried, but this means the cook doesn't get to sit down. Holding the food briefly in the oven is the next best alternative. Serve with Potato Salad with Roasted Peppers and Sesame Seeds (page 169) or Grapefruit Rice with Chives (page 171) and Carolina Vinegar Slaw (page 182).

**serves 4 as a main course
or 8 as an appetizer**

dipping sauce

¼ cup low-sodium soy sauce

2 tablespoons seasoned rice
    vinegar or lemon juice

2 tablespoons water

2 teaspoons minced peeled
    fresh ginger

1 tablespoon minced
    scallions

1½ pounds large shrimp (at
    least 31 to 40 per pound),
    peeled and deveined

Vegetable oil for frying

1 large egg

1 cup all-purpose flour

1. In a small bowl, stir together the dipping sauce ingredients and reserve at room temperature.

2. To keep the shrimp from curling while frying, bend each shrimp straight, breaking the grain of the flesh on the inside curve. Or make 2 or 3 crosswise slashes in that inside curve.

3. Heat 3 inches of vegetable oil in a heavy pot, flat-bottomed wok, or deep-fryer until it registers between 375°F and 380°F on a deep-fat or candy thermometer.

4. In a medium bowl beat together the egg and 1 cup cold water with a fork until foamy. Add the flour and stir with the fork just until barely combined. The batter should look very lumpy, with some dry flour showing and some liquid visibly separated (see Note).

5. Working with 3 or 4 shrimp at a time, so as not to crowd the pan or drop the temperature of the oil, dip each shrimp in the batter, drop it into the oil, and fry for 1 to 2 minutes until crisp and cooked through. Transfer to a rack set over a pan in a warm oven.

Return the oil to between 375°F and 380°F before frying each batch. Serve the shrimp immediately with the dipping sauce.

Notes: In order to get a light lacy coating on the shrimp, the batter must look awful. It is nearly impossible to undermix the water and flour, but if it is stirred even slightly smooth, it will result in a smooth, thick, boring crust.

Draining the shrimp on a rack, rather than brown paper, keeps them from becoming soggy too quickly.

shrimp, egg, and lemon soup

Avgolemono is a classic Greek soup or sauce made with broth, eggs, and lemon juice. Shrimp is a natural addition to this base, and is right at home floating in the smooth, tangy broth. Serve as an appetizer or a main course with bread and Green Salad with Creamy Mustard Dressing and Sweet and Spicy Pecans (page 184), Spinach Salad with Blue Cheese and Plum Dressing (page 186), or Green Salad with Grapes and Sunflower Seeds (page 187).

makes about 6 cups; serves 4 to 6

5 cups chicken broth

¼ cup rice (long, medium, or
   short grain)

1 bay leaf

¼ to ⅓ cup fresh lemon juice

3 large eggs

½ pound shrimp, peeled

(if large, cut into ½-inch
   pieces)

¼ cup chopped fresh dill

Freshly ground black pepper

1. In a large saucepan, combine the broth, rice, and bay leaf; bring to a boil, stirring constantly. Simmer, covered, for 15 minutes, or until the rice is very tender.

2. In a medium bowl, whisk together the lemon juice and eggs, and whisk in about 1 cup of the hot broth in a stream. Whisk the mixture into the remaining broth, add the shrimp, and heat over moderately low heat, stirring constantly, until the broth is hot and slightly thickened, and the shrimp is cooked through. *Do not* let the liquid boil or the eggs will curdle. Stir in the dill and pepper to taste and serve immediately, or chill to serve it cold.

Notes: This soup is fabulous served cold. As it is tricky to reheat, serve any leftovers ice cold, garnished with a little extra dill.

Fresh parsley, cilantro, basil, mint, or tarragon can all replace the dill. Choose your favorite or try a combination.

crab

As with so many things in life, crab preferences are usually established by what you know and what your mom fed you. But with today's modern methods of transportation, the crab boundaries have blurred, and markets offer many more choices than just your local species. When recipes in this chapter call for crabmeat, use whichever picked crab you prefer.

blue crab

This is the crab of the Chesapeake and "Maryland Crab Cakes," though it is caught up and down the eastern seaboard, in Louisiana, and in Texas. Today most of the crabs caught in the Chesapeake area are sold live and consumed locally, while most of the crabmeat consumed nationally is imported and pasteurized.

Pasteurized blue crab can be of excellent quality, but even when it is canned, remember it is perishable and should be refrigerated, and once opened should be eaten within 48 hours. Phillips is one company that uses black lights to expose bits of cartilage when picking crab, leaving their products nearly cartilage free.

Avoid cheap shelf-stable canned crab, which has tiny pieces of crab and is full of cartilage bits.

picked blue crabmeat is categorized
by where it is found on the crab.

Lump and Jumbo Lump: The most expensive and luxurious type, this crab is in large pieces from the meaty large backfin. Use it in salads or sautés where little cooking is involved. Sometimes extravagant crab cakes are made with only lump, but they tend to fall apart easily.

Backfin: This crab is a mixture of small pieces of fin meat and smaller pieces of lump meat. It is a good choice for crab cakes and salads.

Special: This is a mixture of crabmeat from the body, fins, and claws. The pieces are small but flavorful and suitable for fritters, soups, casseroles, and even crab cakes.

Claw: Meat from crab claws has an orange exterior, making it attractive for salads, soups, dips, casseroles, and yes, even crab cakes. Its texture is not as silky as lump, but its flavor is good.

general serving sizes
4 to 6 ounces picked crabmeat per person
1 to 2 pounds live crab in the shell per person

Live crabs are fast and feisty, and can be dangerous if not handled with caution. Once steamed, they should be picked apart one at a time by the diner. Start early and take your time, as this is slow eating at its best. Obviously the smaller the crab, the harder the picking, so reach for the plump ones. It takes a while to get the hang of cracking through the claws and separating the cartilage to extract delectable chunks of sweet meat, but the challenge is part of the satisfaction.

Soft-Shell Crabs: In order for crabs to grow larger, they must molt. That is, they shed their shell as a new one forms underneath. The new, larger shell begins to harden immediately after the old shell has been shed, which is why soft-shells must be removed from the water as soon as they molt.

These delicacies, available fresh from April through September, are eaten whole, shell and all. They should be bought live (they are very docile) and, ideally, cleaned just before cooking. Follow the directions below, ask your fish seller to show you how, or if you just can't stand to do it, have him clean them for you, but you will sacrifice some flavor and juices by cleaning them ahead of time. Frozen soft-shells are okay for frying, but they don't have nearly the flavor or texture of fresh.

TO CLEAN SOFT-SHELL CRABS

1. With a sharp knife or scissors cut off the face and eyes in a thin strip.
2. Turn the crab on its back and pull off its apron—the flap on its underbelly. The apron tells you whether you are eating a male "Jimmy" or a female "sook." Sooks' aprons are rounded with a small point at the end, and Jimmys' are enlongated.
3. Turn the crab over, gently fold back each side of the top shell, and pull off the spongy lungs from both sides of the back.

Dungeness: This large, meaty, sweet crab of the West Coast can be bought live, cooked in the shell, in sections or clusters, picked and frozen, or picked and pasteurized. The average whole crab weighs about 2 pounds, yielding ½ pound picked meat. It is still hard to find Dungeness crab outside of its native region (especially picked meat), but its popularity and distribution is rapidly spreading.

Maine or Jonah Crab: In 1998, when my fish market first tried to sell me Maine crab as a cheaper but equally tasty substitution for blue crab, I was skeptical. But I learned that though it does not have the silky texture of lump crabmeat, it has good flavor and the texture of claw meat.

Peekytoe is another crab from Maine that has gained popularity in upscale restaurants for its sweet flavor and delicate texture, as well as its funky name.

King, Stone, and Snow crab are usually sold fresh or frozen as legs or clusters, and rarely sold as picked meat. However, it is easy to retrieve the meat from the shells.

All picked crabmeat should be checked for pieces of cartilage and shell. Good-quality blue crabmeat should be virtually free of cartilage.

crab, tomato, and basil cocktail

U*se the best crabmeat you can find, and show it off in this refreshing appetizer with dazzling seasonal produce.*

serves 4

½ pound premium crabmeat,
   checked for pieces of
   cartilage

½ cup red cherry tomatoes,
   quartered

½ cup yellow cherry
   tomatoes, quartered

¼ cup thinly sliced scallions
   (a.k.a. green onions)

1 tablespoon fresh lemon
   juice

¼ cup thinly sliced fresh basil
   leaves

Freshly ground black pepper

4 whole Boston lettuce
   leaves, washed and
   spun dry

Toss all of the ingredients together to combine, breaking up the crabmeat as little as possible. Season with black pepper and serve in a lettuce leaf on a chilled plate.

Note: For an hors d'oeuvre, the crab salad can be spooned into small tortilla chip cups or scoops. Garnish each with a small basil leaf or slice of cherry tomato.

hot crab and artichoke filo tartlets

If you have ever tried to individually stack filo, brush it with butter, cut out rounds, and fit it into baking cups, then you will appreciate convenient prebaked, frozen filo cups. Filled with this delicious crab dip, they make it look like you slaved over these hors d'oeuvres.

makes 30 hors d'oeuvres

4 ounces cream cheese

¼ cup mayonnaise

3 scallions (a.k.a. green
 onions)

1 teaspoon Worcestershire
 sauce

¼ cup grated Parmesan

½ cup fine-quality crabmeat,
 checked for pieces of
 cartilage

3 canned artichoke hearts,
 drained and chopped
 (about ¾ cup)

30 frozen mini filo shells
 (2 boxes)

1. Preheat the oven to 400°F.

2. In a medium bowl cream together the cream cheese and mayonnaise until smooth. Stir in the scallions, Worcestershire sauce, and Parmesan. Fold in the crabmeat and artichokes and add salt and pepper to taste.

The filling can be made 1 day in advance, covered, and refrigerated.

3. Fill the filo shells and bake 15 to 20 minutes, until bubbly.

hot crab and spinach dip

Super Bowl party, Christmas open house, graduation, potluck; you name it and this dip should be there. Serve with pita or bagel crisps, sliced baguette, or crackers.

serves 8 to 10

10 ounces fresh spinach, cleaned, or frozen spinach

8 ounces cream cheese

½ cup grated Parmesan

¾ cup mayonnaise

2 tablespoons fresh lemon juice

1 tablespoon Worcestershire sauce

½ teaspoon salt

½ teaspoon pepper

⅓ cup minced onions

1 pound fine-quality crabmeat, checked for pieces of cartilage

½ cup sliced almonds

1. Preheat the oven to 375°F. Butter a shallow 6-cup baking dish.

2. In a saucepan, bring 1 cup water to a boil. Add the fresh or frozen spinach and cook, covered, for 3 minutes. Drain and rinse briefly under cold water. Squeeze the spinach dry by handfuls.

3. In a food processor blend the cream cheese, Parmesan, mayonnaise, lemon juice, Worcestershire sauce, salt, and pepper. Add the spinach and onion and pulse the motor until the spinach is chopped but not pureed.

4. Transfer the mixture to the prepared baking dish and fold in the crabmeat. Smooth the dip and sprinkle with the almonds.

The dip can be made 1 day in advance, covered, and refrigerated.

5. Bake until bubbling and golden, about 25 minutes (30 to 40 minutes if chilled). Serve hot.

crab hush puppies with old bay dip

Serve these chunky crab and corn treats hot from the pan as hors d'oeuvres or as a part of a seafood feast.

makes about 20

½ cup yellow cornmeal

½ teaspoon baking powder

½ teaspoon salt

½ cup canned creamed-style
   corn

1 large egg yolk

¼ cup chopped scallions
   (a.k.a. green onions)

½ pound crabmeat, checked
   for pieces of cartilage

Vegetable oil for frying

Old Bay Dip (recipe follows)

Honey mustard as an
   accompaniment

1. In a large bowl, whisk together the cornmeal, baking powder, and salt. Add the creamed corn, egg yolk, and scallions, and stir to form a batter. Gently stir in the crabmeat and let the batter rest for 15 minutes.

2. In a large skillet, heat 1 inch of oil until it registers 350°F on a deep-fat thermometer. Drop walnut-sized scoops of the batter into the oil and cook for 1 to 2 minutes on each side, or until browned and cooked through. Remove with a slotted spoon and transfer them to brown paper to drain, and keep warm in a 250°F oven for up to 20 minutes until ready to serve.

3. Serve with the dip or honey mustard.

old bay dip

½ cup sour cream

1 tablespoon Old Bay
   Seasoning

2 teaspoons fresh lemon juice

In a small bowl, stir together the sour cream, Old Bay Seasoning, and lemon juice, and refrigerate until ready to serve.

sesame crab salad with cucumbers, radishes, and snow peas

Composed salads, which are arranged on individual plates, are an easy way to make simple ingredients look elegant. To save time, I serve one large salad on a platter, overlapping the cucumbers and radishes in rings, with the crab in the middle, and let people serve themselves. This eye-catching, crunchy Asian-flavored salad can be served as is for lunch, or a light supper, served with warm pita bread.

serves 4

1 medium cucumber

1½ cups clean, trimmed radishes (1 bunch)

¼ pound fresh snow peas, trimmed

¼ cup rice vinegar

½ teaspoon salt

½ teaspoon sugar

¼ cup vegetable oil

1 teaspoon Asian toasted sesame oil

2 tablespoons minced scallions (a.k.a. green onions)

½ pound fine-quality crabmeat, checked for pieces of cartilage

1 teaspoon sesame seeds

1. Peel the cucumber, leaving some skin on in stripes. With a food processor fitted with a thin slicing disk, or a handheld slicer, cut the cucumber into thin slices. Slice the radishes in the same way and set aside.

2. In a saucepan of boiling salted water, blanch the snow peas for 1 to 2 minutes, or until they are crisp-tender. Drain in a colander and rinse under cold water. Slice the snow peas crosswise into ¼-inch-wide pieces.

3. In a small bowl, whisk together the vinegar, salt, sugar, vegetable oil, sesame oil, and scallions until emulsified. In a medium bowl toss the crabmeat and snow peas with 2 tablespoons of the dressing, and season with pepper to taste.

4. Arrange the cucumber slices, overlapping, around the edge of a platter. Scatter the radish slices in a ring inside the cucumbers and pile the crab mixture in the middle.

5. Drizzle the remaining dressing over everything and sprinkle with the sesame seeds.

crab and avocado salad
with grapefruit honey dressing

This light, refreshing salad is a perfect one-dish lunch. For supper, add Summer Corn on the Cob with Basil Butter (page 175) and Grapefruit Rice with Chives (page 171).

serves 2

2 teaspoons light-colored
   honey

1/4 cup fresh grapefruit juice

1 tablespoon wine vinegar

1/4 cup olive oil

1/2 pound fine-quality
   crabmeat, checked for
   pieces of cartilage

1 small orange or yellow bell
   pepper, diced

1/4 cup chopped red onions

1 ripe avocado

1. In a large bowl, dissolve the honey in the grapefruit juice and vinegar, whisking. Add the oil and whisk until well blended. Add the crabmeat, bell pepper, onions, and salt and pepper to taste and toss.

2. Peel, pit, and slice the avocado. Divide the slices among four plates and top with the crab salad.

baked curried crab toasts

A *crab salad seasoned with chiles, curry powder, lime juice, and cilantro is piled on bread, topped with coconut, and baked to a golden brown. This dish is like a crab cake, but its bread base makes it easy to serve as a finger food as well as an impressive main course. To make a meal, serve the toasts with Red, White, and Blue Slaw (page 183) and Sliced Asparagus and Edamame with Olive Oil (page 176).*

serves 4 as a main course
or 8 as an appetizer

4 slices wheat or white
  sandwich bread

¼ cup mayonnaise

1 large egg yolk

1 teaspoon minced fresh hot
  chile, including the seeds
  (such as habanero, serrano,
  or Thai), or ¼ teaspoon hot
  red pepper flakes

¼ cup finely chopped
  scallions (a.k.a. green
  onions)

¼ cup chopped fresh cilantro

1 teaspoon curry powder

1 tablespoon fresh lime juice

½ pound fine-quality
  crabmeat, checked for
  pieces of cartilage

⅓ cup sweetened flaked
  coconut

1. Preheat the oven to 400°F.

2. Cut the crusts from the bread and in a food processor or blender finely grind the crusts.

3. In a large bowl, stir together ⅓ cup of the bread crumbs (save the remaining crumbs for another use), the mayonnaise, egg yolk, chile, scallions, cilantro, curry powder, and lime juice. Stir in the crabmeat and salt to taste.

4. Divide the crab mixture among the bread slices, spreading it to the edges, and put them on a baking sheet. Top the crab with the coconut, pressing it on to adhere.

The toasts can be prepared up to this point 2 hours in advance, covered, and refrigerated.

5. Bake the toasts in the middle of the oven until golden and puffed, 20 to 25 minutes. Cut each toast in quarters and serve immediately.

crab and goat cheese frittata

*T*his open-faced omelet can be served for brunch, lunch, or as a light supper. Sprouts and Sliced Tomato Salad (page 179), Carolina Vinegar Slaw (page 182), or just a simple green salad would complement it well.

serves 4

½ cup chopped onions

½ cup finely chopped celery

1 tablespoon butter

6 large eggs, beaten with a
   fork

½ pound fine-quality
   crabmeat, checked for
   pieces of cartilage

3 ounces soft mild goat
   cheese

¼ cup shredded mozzarella
   or Swiss cheese

3 tablespoons chopped
   chives

Freshly ground black pepper

1. In a 10-inch nonstick skillet (measuring across the top), cook the onion and celery in the butter over moderate heat, stirring, until softened, about 10 minutes. Add the eggs, stirring to distribute the vegetables evenly, and cook for 1 minute.

2. With a rubber spatula, pull the set egg mixture away from the side of the pan, tilting it to allow uncooked egg to flow underneath. Do this all around the edges until most of the egg is set but it is still wet on top. Sprinkle the top with the crabmeat and cheeses. Reduce the heat slightly, cover the pan, and cook the frittata until the cheese is melted, 3 to 5 minutes.

3. Run the rubber spatula around the frittata and slide it onto a plate. Sprinkle with the chives and freshly ground black pepper. Cut into wedges and serve immediately.

steamed spiced blue crabs

In the mid-Atlantic United States, when someone asks, "Do you want to eat crabs?" they mean blue crabs cooked this way. From spring through fall, steamed crabs are eaten from trucks along the road-side, and piled high on brown paper–lined tables in crab shacks and restaurants. A favorite summer-time feast in my house is crabs and ribs. We start early because you need time to pick crab at your own pace, fill in the spaces with a pork rib or two, and cool off your throat with some ice cold beer and lemonade. A crab feast is the best way I know to slow people down and remind them what fun it is to laze around, eat with your hands, and shoot the breeze. Plus, it is nearly impossible to answer a cell phone when your hands are covered in spices and barbecue sauce.

serves 4

¼ cup white vinegar

24 live hard-shell blue crabs

1 onion, thinly sliced

½ cup Old Bay Seasoning

1. Set a steaming rack, such as an expandable vegetable steamer, in the bottom of a large pot. Add the vinegar and 2 inches of water and bring to a boil.

2. Add half the crabs, carefully (they are feisty), and sprinkle with half the onion and half the seasoning. Add the remaining crabs, onion, and seasoning, and cover tightly.

3. Steam the crabs over high heat for 18 minutes and remove the pot from the heat. Pour off the cooking liquid.

4. The crabs can be served directly from the pot, or piled on a paper-lined table.

tools

Wooden mallets, metal claw crackers, and metal skewers are
necessary tools for picking the crab.

TO PICK A CRAB

1. Turn the crab on its back and pull off its apron—the flap on its
   underbelly. The apron tells you whether you are eating a male
   "Jimmy" or a female "sook." Sooks' aprons are rounded with a
   small point at the end, and Jimmys' are elongated.
2. Turn the crab over and pull off the large back shell. The yellow
   stuff inside is called mustard, and can be eaten, ignored, or
   scraped away. Any hard, red bumpy-looking stuff is roe, which
   can also be eaten or discarded.
3. Pull off the spongy lungs from both sides of the back.
4. Break off the large claws, crack them, and pick out the meat.
5. Break the crab in half and work with one half at a time. Each of
   the small claws leads to a lump of meat where it attaches to the
   body. Each of the lumps is surrounded by a thin cartilage. If you
   wiggle and pull the claw from the body, sometimes the whole
   lump will come out attached to the leg. Otherwise, crack the
   body cavities, picking out the prized sweet white flesh.

crab cakes with orange chive mayonnaise

Crab cakes can be an intense, memorable crab-tasting experience, or they can be bready crab-flavored fried patties. I don't believe you have to use all lump blue crabmeat to make the best crab cakes, which often are overly rich and fall apart easily. But they should be almost entirely crabmeat with the least amount of binding ingredients possible. Balance out the richness with Carolina Vinegar Slaw (page 182) and Sliced Asparagus and Edamame with Olive Oil (page 176).

makes 4 cakes; serves 2

½ cup chopped onions

½ cup chopped green bell
   pepper

5 tablespoons butter

2 tablespoons mayonnaise

1 tablespoon Worcestershire
   sauce

1 tablespoon Dijon mustard

1 large egg yolk

½ teaspoon freshly ground
   black pepper

8 saltine crackers, crushed

½ pound backfin blue crab or
   other fine-quality crabmeat,
   checked for pieces of
   cartilage

2 tablespoons vegetable oil

Orange Chive Mayonnaise
   (recipe follows) or tartar
   sauce as an
   accompaniment

1. In a medium skillet, cook the onion and bell pepper in 3 tablespoons of the butter over moderate heat, stirring, until limp, about 5 minutes. Transfer to a large bowl and stir in the mayonnaise, Worcestershire sauce, mustard, egg yolk, pepper, and cracker crumbs.

2. Add the crabmeat and stir gently to combine the mixture, keeping the crab lumps intact. Press the mixture into 4 patties about 1 inch thick and put on a plate. Chill the patties, covered, for 30 minutes to help them hold together.

The cakes can be made up to 8 hours in advance, covered, and chilled.

3. Heat the remaining 2 tablespoons butter and the oil in a large skillet over moderate heat. Add the crab cakes and cook until golden brown, about 4 minutes on each side. Serve immediately with the mayonnaise.

orange chive
mayonnaise

makes about ½ cup

¼ cup mayonnaise

2 tablespoons orange juice

2 tablespoons minced chives

1 to 2 teaspoons Tabasco or

　other hot pepper sauce

Combine all the ingredients in a bowl, adding Tabasco to taste, cover, and chill until ready to serve.

crab roasted in tomato shells

Make this in the summer when good vine-ripened tomatoes are available. Serve for brunch, lunch, or dinner with Orange Orzo with Basil (page 167), Sliced Asparagus and Edamame with Olive Oil (page 176), and a simple salad or slaw.

serves 4

½ pound fine-quality crabmeat, checked for pieces of cartilage

⅓ cup thinly sliced scallions (a.k.a. green onions)

½ cup chopped celery

⅓ cup mayonnaise

1½ cups shredded Gruyère (about ¼ pound)

¼ cup chopped fresh parsley

4 medium tomatoes

1. Preheat the oven to 450°F.

2. In a large bowl gently toss together the crabmeat, scallions, celery, mayonnaise, 1 cup of the Gruyère, the parsley, and salt and pepper to taste.

3. Cut out the stem end of each tomato, and scoop out the inside flesh and seeds. Fill the tomato shells with the crab mixture, top with the remaining Gruyère, and put in a shallow baking pan or dish.

4. Roast the tomatoes for 25 minutes, or until heated through. Serve immediately.

Note: Alternatively, the crab mixture can be baked in individual ramekins or gratin dishes, or in one large baking dish to serve as an hors d'oeuvre. Serve with a sprinkle of lemon juice, to make up for the tartness of the tomato.

crab pasta primavera

The springtime classic Pasta Primavera makes use of whatever tender young vegetables are at the market. But you can use any vegetables in any season along with crabmeat to make this special dish any time of year. This is really a one-dish meal, but Eggless Caesar Salad (page 188) and garlic bread are always welcome alongside.

serves 4

2 leeks, washed well and
  thinly sliced (see Note)

2 large garlic cloves, minced

3 tablespoons olive oil

1 tablespoon all-purpose flour

¾ cup dry white wine or
  vermouth

1 cup bottled clam juice or
  shell stock (see page 4)

1 teaspoon hot red pepper
  flakes (optional)

2 tablespoons fresh tarragon
  or 1 teaspoon dried
  tarragon

½ cup heavy cream

¾ pound linguine

¾ pound asparagus, washed,
  trimmed, and cut into
  ½-inch pieces

2 cups fresh or frozen peas

½ pound fine-quality
  crabmeat, checked for
  pieces of cartilage

1. In a large, deep skillet, cook the leeks and garlic in the oil over moderately low heat, covered, stirring occasionally, until softened, about 15 minutes. Add the flour and cook, stirring, for 1 minute. Add the wine, clam juice, pepper flakes (if using), tarragon (if using dried), and salt to taste, and simmer for 10 minutes. Stir in the cream.

2. Meanwhile, in a large pot of boiling salted water, cook the linguine for 3 minutes less than the manufacturer's directions. Add the asparagus to the pot and boil for 1 minute. Add the peas and boil 2 minutes more, or until the pasta is tender and the vegetables are crisp-tender.

3. Drain the linguine well in a colander, and immediately add to the sauce in the skillet, with the crabmeat. Toss well and sprinkle with the tarragon (if using fresh).

Note: It is very important to wash leeks well as they tend to hold dirt between their leaves. Trim the tough dark green leaves from the leeks. Split them lengthwise, leaving them attached at the root end, and rinse them thoroughly under running water, separating the leaves to wash away any grit.

crabmeat sautéed with prosciutto

This recipe comes from my friend Margaret, who grew up in Baltimore, Maryland. As her two-year-old son sat on her lap and devoured her portion of precious lump crabmeat, she knew she would pay, literally, for encouraging such expensive tastes in a child so young. It can be served over plain rice or with Orange Orzo with Basil (page 167), Jollof Rice (page 168), or Baked Vegetable and Cheese Polenta (page 174).

serves 4 as a first course
and 2 as a main course

2 tablespoons butter

2 very thin slices prosciutto
or other fine-quality ham

½ pound lump blue crab or
other large pieces of
fine-quality crabmeat
(see Note)

2 teaspoons fresh lemon juice

Freshly ground black pepper

In a small, heavy skillet, heat the butter over moderately high heat. Add the prosciutto and cook, stirring, for 1 minute, or until it begins to crisp. Add the crabmeat and cook, tossing gently until it is heated through, about 2 minutes. Remove the pan from the heat and sprinkle with the lemon juice and pepper to taste. Serve immediately.

Note: Because this dish is basically warmed crab, you will want to use the best, meatiest crab pieces you can buy. Lump or jumbo lump blue crab or picked Dungeness or king crab are worthy of starring in this dish.

soft-shell crabs sautéed in garlic butter

Once you have made your own soft-shell crabs at home, ordering them out will always be a letdown. Be careful of spattering oil as the crabs cook and give off juices. Serve with Mom's Coleslaw (page 181), Two Potato Hash (page 170), or Celery and Lima Bean Puree (page 173).

serves 4

8 soft-shell crabs, cleaned
(see page 40)

1 cup milk

½ cup all-purpose flour,
seasoned with salt and
pepper

2 tablespoons butter

2 tablespoons olive oil

2 large garlic cloves,
quartered

Lemon wedges

1. In a large bowl soak the crabs in the milk in the refrigerator for 30 minutes to 3 hours.

2. Dredge the crabs in flour. Heat 1 tablespoon each of the butter and oil with the garlic in a large, heavy skillet over moderate heat until it sizzles, and in it fry four of the crabs until golden brown, about 4 minutes on each side. Repeat with the remaining butter, oil, and crabs.

3. Serve with lemon wedges.

soft-shell crabs on arepas (cornmeal patties)

This dish combines some of my favorite tastes. A crisp-on-the-outside soft-on-the-inside Colombian cornmeal cake, or arepa, is topped with a crisp and juicy soft-shell crab. A light sweet-and-sour slaw washes over the richness, creating an ideal mix of flavors and textures. This is really an entire meal in itself, but Quick Pickled Green Beans (page 178) or Carrot Ribbons with Lemon and Cumin (page 180) could be served alongside.

serves 4

8 large soft-shell crabs,
    cleaned (see page 40)
1 to 2 cups milk

for the arepas

¾ cup corn masa (fine
    cornmeal; see Note)
¼ cup freshly grated
    Parmesan
¾ teaspoon salt
¼ to ⅓ cup vegetable oil

for frying the crabs

½ cup all-purpose flour,
    seasoned with salt and
    pepper
2 tablespoons butter
2 tablespoons olive oil
Carolina Vinegar Slaw
    (page 182)

1. Combine the crabs and enough milk to cover in a large bowl. Let them soak while preparing the arepas.

2. In a small bowl, stir together the corn masa, ¾ cup water, the Parmesan, and salt until a loose dough is formed that resembles wet sand or mud. Heat 1 teaspoon of the vegetable oil in a small nonstick skillet or well-seasoned cast-iron skillet over moderately high heat. With dampened hands, pat one-fourth of the dough into a round, passing it back and forth between your hands like making a mud pie, until it is about ¼ inch thick. Add the arepa to the skillet and fry until golden, 3 to 5 minutes. Turn the arepa, adding more oil, if necessary, and cook 3 to 5 minutes more, reducing the heat if it cooks too fast. Transfer to a baking sheet and keep warm in a 200°F oven until ready to serve. Make three more arepas in the same manner.

3. Dredge the crabs in flour. Heat 1 tablespoon each of the butter and olive oil in a large, heavy skillet over moderate heat until it sizzles, and in it fry four of the crabs until golden brown, about 4 minutes on each side. Repeat with the remaining butter, oil, and crabs.

4. To serve, arrange two crabs on an arepa on a dinner plate, and top with some of the slaw.

Note: Arepas are crisp-fried cornmeal cakes from Colombia, South America. Like pupusas, tamales, and thick fresh corn tortillas, they are made from fine cornmeal, either yellow or white, often found in the international section of supermarkets or Latino markets. The best way to identify the cornmeal, which is ground finer than regular cornmeal but not as fine as corn flour, is if its package has directions for making arepas, pupusas, or tamales.

cream of crab soup

Thick, rich, and chunky with crab, this soup is pure indulgence. The classic flavor of sherry adds just the right sweetness to balance the silky cream. Serve as an appetizer or luncheon main course with bread and Green Salad with Creamy Mustard Dressing and Sweet and Spicy Pecans (page 184) or Green Salad with Grapes and Sunflower Seeds (page 187).

makes about 6½ cups;
serves 4 to 6

1 small onion, chopped
 (about 1 cup)

1 cup chopped celery (about
 2 ribs)

½ stick (4 tablespoons butter)

1 bay leaf

⅓ cup all-purpose flour

2 cups bottled clam juice,
 chicken broth, or shell
 stock (see page 4)

1 teaspoon dried thyme

2 cups heavy cream

⅓ cup sherry

1 tablespoon Dijon mustard

1 pound crabmeat, checked
 for pieces of cartilage

Paprika for garnish

1. In a large, heavy saucepan, cook the onion and celery in the butter with the bay leaf over moderate heat, stirring, until softened, about 15 minutes.

2. Stir in the flour and cook, stirring, for 2 minutes. Add the clam juice and thyme, and simmer, whisking, for 5 minutes. Add the cream, sherry, and mustard, and bring to a boil, whisking.

3. Stir in the crabmeat and salt and pepper to taste, and bring to a boil. Ladle the soup into bowls, discarding the bay leaf, and sprinkle with paprika.

gingered butternut squash and crab soup

Smooth, warm, and comforting with a bite of ginger and seductive chunks of crab, this soup is one of my favorites. It is impressive as a first course, and satisfying as a supper with a loaf of crusty bread. For a meal, serve it with Spinach Salad with Blue Cheese and Plum Dressing (page 186).

makes about 6 cups: serves 4 to 6

2 pounds butternut squash or calabaza (see Note)

1 medium onion, chopped (about 1½ cups)

½ stick (4 tablespoons) butter

2 cups bottled clam juice or shell stock (see page 4)

3 tablespoons coarsely grated peeled fresh ginger (about a 3-inch piece)

1 teaspoon salt

¼ teaspoon pepper

2 tablespoons fresh lime juice

½ pound fine-quality crabmeat, checked for pieces of cartilage

Chopped basil, cilantro, and croutons for garnish (optional)

1. Halve the squash, scoop out the seeds, and peel with a vegetable peeler. Cut the squash into ½-inch cubes; there should be about 5 cups.

2. Cook the onion in the butter in a heavy pot or deep skillet over moderate heat for 5 minutes. Add the squash and cook, stirring occasionally, for 10 minutes, or until the squash is aromatic and beginning to soften. Add the clam juice, ginger, salt, and pepper and simmer, covered, for 10 minutes, or until the squash is easily mashed with a fork.

3. Puree the soup in a blender or food processor in batches and return to the pot. Stir in the lime juice and crabmeat.

   The soup can be made a day ahead, covered and refrigerated, or frozen for 3 months. (Let cool, uncovered, before freezing.)

4. Serve the soup hot with suggested garnishes, if desired.

Note: Calabaza is a bright orange–fleshed pumpkin common to Latin American and West Indian cuisine, and becoming more and more available in supermarkets across the United States. Because it is a large vegetable, it is usually sold in halves or chunks. Its deep egg-yolk color, sweet flavor, and smooth texture make it perfect for this soup.

chilled crab, cucumber, and avocado soup

This cold soup is perfect for a hot summer day and hearty enough for a crisp autumn day. The optional mango garnish adds a beautiful contrasting color as well as a refreshing sweet flavor.

makes about 3½ cups;
serves 4 as a first course

½ cup plain yogurt or sour cream

1 cucumber, peeled, seeded, and chopped (about 1 cup)

1 ripe Hass avocado, peeled and pitted

1 tablespoon fresh tarragon or 1 teaspoon dried tarragon

½ teaspoon ground cumin

1 small garlic clove

1 cup bottled clam juice or shell stock (see page 4)

½ pound fine-quality crabmeat, checked for pieces of cartilage

Finely chopped mango for garnish (optional)

1. In a blender puree the yogurt, half the cucumber, the avocado, tarragon, cumin, garlic, and ½ cup of the clam juice. Add enough additional clam juice to reach the desired consistency. Transfer to a medium bowl and stir in the crabmeat, remaining cucumber, and salt and pepper to taste.

2. Serve cold, topped with the mango, if desired.

scallops

sea scallops

Harvested from deep ocean waters, the sea scallop's single, sweet, buttery muscle is what is consumed, while the rest of the mollusk is discarded. Sea scallops can range from 1 inch to almost 3 inches in diameter (10 to 20 per pound).

Many classic recipes have you remove the slightly tough small muscle that is attached to the side of each scallop. In most cases I think this is a waste, because while the little nugget may have a slightly tough texture, its flavor is good. I leave it up to personal preference.

bay scallops

As their name implies, these scallops are harvested in the shallow waters of bays. Because of their proximity to land and problems with pollution and red tide, the prized fresh bay scallops of Long Island, Cape Cod, and Nova Scotia are a rare and expensive delicacy. At their best, bay scallops are plump and creamy colored with the best sweet, nutty flavor of any scallop, and are the size of a large thumbnail. Some overseas producers are having success raising Peconic Bay scallops, which are available frozen, but most of the bay scallops available in supermarkets are the tiny (the size of a pinkie nail), tough, and tasteless calico scallops.

The most important thing to understand about buying any scallops is that there is a difference between the taste and texture of scallops that have been soaked in tripolyphosphate solution and those that have not.

"**Wet**" scallops, which have been treated with tripolyphosphate preservative solution (and account for the majority of scallops in the market), appear very shiny and white. They also do not hold their shape distinctly separate from one another, and they are more likely to pull apart. These scallops are frustrating to use in kebabs, as skewers tend to pull right through them. The preserving solution also causes them to absorb water, making them heavier at purchase. As a result, they shrink when cooked, and the release of so much liquid makes it hard to get a lovely seared crust on the sides. The sweet natural flavor of the scallop is also clouded by a slight aftertaste similar to baking soda.

"**Dry**" scallops (those that have not been soaked) appear firmer and milkier in color, though still shiny. These scallops are usually marked "dry" or "untreated" in the market because the vendors want people to know why they are a little more expensive. Any fish salesperson should be able to tell you if their scallops are "wet" or "dry."

Some frozen scallops can be of very good quality when they are flash-frozen on the boat, making preservatives unnecessary. I have bought delicious frozen sea and bay scallops at warehouse markets such as Costco, as well as at some supermarkets. Look at the ingredients listing on frozen packages. If a preservative solution was used, it will be listed, otherwise "scallops" should be the only ingredient.

"**Diver**" scallops refer to scallops that are harvested by hand by deep-sea divers. These are obviously the most expensive, and are mostly sought after by high-end restaurants, which usually serve them the day they are caught. For this reason, they are sometimes called "Day" or "Day Boat" scallops.

Pink scallops are beautiful delicacies sold in the shell, which is a beautiful pale rose. They are steamed in their shells until the creamy bay scallop muscle is exposed, with its delicate pink roe attached. One meal I will never forget was at Ray's Boathouse on Shilshole Bay in Seattle, where I feasted on their "Singing Scallops." The name comes either from the way the scallops look when arranged in a bowl with the open ends up, or from what they make you want to do while eating them. If you have a chance to try this rare treat, don't pass it up.

seared sesame sea scallops with wasabi vinaigrette

This is an elegant and sophisticated way to prepare scallops, and also one of the easiest. The key to obtaining a golden seared crust on each scallop is having a heavy nonstick pan, dry scallops, and giving them room in the pan so they don't steam. The vinaigrette offers a clean, slightly acidic foil to the richness of the scallop. Suitable partners on the side are Orange Orzo with Basil (page 167) and Sliced Asparagus and Edamame with Olive Oil (page 176).

**serves 4 as a main course
or 6 as an appetizer**

for the vinaigrette

2 teaspoons wasabi paste or
   1 tablespoon wasabi
   powder mixed with
   1 teaspoon water
3 tablespoons low-sodium
   soy sauce
3 tablespoons seasoned rice
   vinegar
3 tablespoons vegetable oil
1 teaspoon sugar
2 teaspoons minced peeled
   fresh ginger

1½ pounds sea scallops,
   rinsed if gritty
About 2 tablespoons
   vegetable oil
2 tablespoons sesame seeds

1. In a medium bowl, whisk together all of the vinaigrette ingredients, and let stand at room temperature until ready to serve.

2. Pat the scallops dry and season lightly with salt and pepper.

3. Heat 1 tablespoon of the oil in a large, heavy nonstick skillet over moderate heat, and add the scallops in a single layer, in batches if necessary, leaving space around each scallop. Cook for 3 to 5 minutes, turn the scallops, and add the sesame seeds (during the last batch only). Cook another 3 to 5 minutes, or until just cooked through.

4. Divide the scallops among plates, sprinkle with the sesame seeds, and drizzle with the vinaigrette.

scallop seviche

Seviche is a Spanish term that refers to "cooking" raw fish in an acidic base such as lime juice, lemon juice, or vinegar. The most memorable seviche I have had was in Mexico, while fishing off the coast of a small island called Contoy. After landing a large barracuda fish on the deck of our small fishing boat, the captain proceeded to fillet, skin, chop, and mix it with the basic Mexican seviche ingredients: lime juice, habanero chile, tomato, and cilantro, all of which magically appeared from under one of the seats. He also whipped up a perfect guacamole and pulled out a bag of recently fried corn tortilla chips. I am not sure I will ever be able to re-create that dish, because certainly the circumstances contributed to its memorable flavor, and fresh, edible barracuda is hard to come by, but the recipe below is a close replica. Tortilla chips are still a perfect accompaniment.

serves 4 to 6

1½ pounds sea scallops, rinsed if gritty and sliced into very thin rounds (see Note)

1 cup cherry tomatoes, sliced into thin rounds

⅓ cup fresh lime juice

¼ cup chopped red onions

½ teaspoon salt

3 tablespoons finely chopped fresh cilantro

1 tablespoon olive or vegetable oil

1 small habanero, serrano, jalapeño, or other hot chile, finely chopped

In a large bowl, stir together all of the ingredients except the chopped chile. Add the chile a little at a time, according to taste. Let the scallops "cook" in the lime juice, covered and refrigerated, for 1 to 3 hours. Serve cold.

Note: It is important to use "dry" scallops, or frozen scallops that have not been treated with preserving chemicals. The tripolyphosphate solution in which "wet" scallops are soaked leaves a slightly bitter, unpleasant aftertaste reminiscent of baking soda, especially when scallops are eaten raw.

chilled lemon and basil-marinated scallops

This dish is like a seviche, where raw seafood is "cooked" by an acidic sauce of vinegar, lemon, or lime juice. However, here the scallops are cooked in oil before being marinated. Serve these as an hors d'oeuvre with crackers, as an appetizer with a sliced baguette, or as a light lunch or supper main course on a bed of greens.

For a varied antipasto, pass the following dishes with the scallops, or choose a couple to make it a meal: Warm Herbed White Bean Salad (page 172), Celery and Lima Bean Puree (page 173), Baked Vegetable and Cheese Polenta (page 174), or Sliced Asparagus and Edamame with Olive Oil (page 176).

serves 4 to 8

1½ pounds sea scallops

½ cup extra virgin olive oil

Zest of 1 lemon, removed
   with a vegetable peeler

2 garlic cloves, halved

1 bay leaf

¼ cup fresh lemon juice

3 tablespoons wine vinegar

¾ teaspoon salt

½ teaspoon sugar

¼ cup finely chopped fresh
   basil

One 7-ounce jar roasted red
   peppers, drained and
   chopped

1. Halve the scallops horizontally into rounds, removing the tough side muscle, and pat them dry.

2. In a large, deep skillet, heat the oil over moderate heat with the lemon zest, garlic, and bay leaf until the zest sizzles, 2 minutes. Add the scallops and cook, stirring, for 2 minutes and remove the pan from the heat. Stir in the remaining ingredients.

3. Transfer the scallops in the marinade to a glass or ceramic bowl, cover, and refrigerate for at least 4 hours or overnight. Serve cold.

cornbread-crusted scallops
with chipotle tartar sauce

Cornbread stuffing mix provides a crisp and flavorful coating for delicate, sweet sea scallops. The spicy tartar sauce can be used on any fish or shellfish, and also makes a nice cocktail sauce for cold shrimp. Serve colorful vegetables alongside to balance the flavors, such as Carrot Ribbons with Lemon and Cumin (page 180), Red, White, and Blue Slaw (page 183), or Quick Pickled Green Beans (page 178).

serves 4

½ cup mayonnaise

2 tablespoons fresh lime juice

1½ tablespoons minced canned chipotles in adobo sauce (see Note)

1 tablespoon sweet pickle relish

2 teaspoons minced fresh parsley

½ cup dry cornbread stuffing mix

1 large egg

1½ pounds sea scallops, patted dry

Vegetable oil for frying

1. In a small bowl, stir together the mayonnaise, lime juice, chipotles, relish, and parsley, and reserve the tartar sauce, covered and chilled.

2. In a blender or food processor, finely grind the stuffing mix and transfer to a bowl.

3. In a medium bowl, beat the egg lightly, add the scallops, and coat well.

4. Heat ½ inch of the oil in a deep skillet over moderate to moderately high heat until it sizzles when some cornbread crumbs are added. Dredge each scallop in the crumbs and fry in the oil for about 1 minute on each side, or until it is golden brown and just cooked through. Drain the scallops on paper towels and serve immediately with the tartar sauce.

Note: Chipotle chiles are smoked red jalapeños, very spicy with a delicious smoky taste. Chipotles in adobo sauce come in small cans. A little goes a long way, so use what you need and freeze the remainder in a small container or a plastic freezer bag.

blackened scallops with
grapefruit sour cream sauce

This is a dish of contrasts: hot and cool; black and white; crisp and soft. Spiced, seared scallops, not burned as "blackened" implies, sit in a cool, creamy grapefruit sauce. Make the sauce and spice mixture in advance, leaving only the scallops to cook at the last minute. Serve with Two Potato Hash (page 170), Carolina Vinegar Slaw (page 182), or Green Salad with Grapes and Sunflower Seeds (page 187).

serves 4

for the sauce

½ cup sour cream

1 teaspoon grated grapefruit
zest

½ cup fresh-squeezed
grapefruit juice

2 teaspoons Dijon mustard

¼ teaspoon salt

1 tablespoon sweet paprika

¾ teaspoon ground coriander

¾ teaspoon ground cumin

¾ teaspoon freshly ground
black pepper

1½ pounds sea scallops

2 tablespoons olive or
vegetable oil

Minced fresh chives or
parsley for garnish
(optional)

1. Make the sauce: In a small bowl, whisk together the sauce ingredients and let stand at room temperature for up to 1 hour.

The sauce can be made up to 4 hours in advance, covered, and refrigerated.

2. In a small bowl, combine the paprika, coriander, cumin, and pepper, and blend together well. Pat the scallops dry with paper towels and dip each end of each scallop in the spice mixture.

3. In a large nonstick skillet, heat the oil over moderate heat until hot. Add the scallops in batches and cook for 3 to 5 minutes on each side, or until they are just cooked through.

4. Pour some of the sauce on four plates and top with the scallops. Garnish with the chives or parsley, if desired.

Note: The trick to getting a nicely browned crust with scallops is to dry them thoroughly just before cooking. If they are too close together in the pan, they will steam rather than sear. If they are browning too fast, reduce the heat to ensure they cook through without burning.

scallop and saffron fettuccine alfredo

Saffron's exotic bittersweet taste and beautiful color give this dish a special flair. The egg adds extra protein as well as a velvety thickness to the sauce. Pasta, of course, screams for a green salad, such as Eggless Caesar Salad (page 188), but Carrot Ribbons with Lemon and Cumin (page 180) can play a refreshing and attractive supporting role.

serves 2 as a main course
or 4 as an appetizer

3 shallots, chopped (about
⅓ cup)

⅛ teaspoon crumbled saffron
threads

1 tablespoon olive oil

⅓ cup dry white wine

½ cup frozen peas, thawed

½ cup heavy cream

1 pound sea scallops, sliced
horizontally into rounds, or
bay scallops

1 large egg, beaten

2 teaspoons chopped fresh
oregano or basil

½ pound fettuccine

1. In a large, heavy skillet, cook the shallots and saffron in the oil over moderate heat for 2 minutes. Add the wine and simmer until it is reduced to about 2 tablespoons. Add the peas and cream and simmer, stirring, for 2 minutes. Add the scallops and simmer for 1 minute, or until barely cooked through.

2. Remove the skillet from the heat, push the solids to one side of the pan, and add the beaten egg in a stream, whisking constantly until incorporated (the sauce will thicken slightly). Add the oregano and salt and pepper to taste.

The dish can be made up to this point about 30 minutes in advance and kept warm, covered.

3. In a pot of salted boiling water, cook the fettuccine until just tender. Drain well and immediately add it to the scallop sauce. Heat the mixture over moderately low heat for about 2 minutes, tossing until it is hot. (Do not let the sauce boil or it will curdle the egg.) Serve immediately.

Note: This is a dish that is suited to many types of shellfish. Try lobster, shrimp, crawfish, crab, squid, or any combination.

noodles with scallops, snow peas, and ginger sauce

I *made this dish years ago when I was lucky enough to be on the East End of Long Island, New York, when native Peconic Bay scallops were in season. I wanted to stretch them to make a meal (as they are expensive but worth every penny), but I didn't want to overwhelm their delicate sweet sea flavor. Ginger, scallion, butter, and wine are perfect partners for these delicacies, as is Summer Corn on the Cob with Basil Butter (page 175) or Sprouts and Sliced Tomato Salad (page 179).*

serves 2 to 3

6 ounces medium egg
noodles

¼ pound snow peas,
trimmed and cut into ½-
inch pieces

½ stick (4 tablespoons) butter

2 tablespoons minced peeled
fresh ginger

½ cup thinly sliced scallions
(a.k.a. green onions)

¾ cup dry white wine

1 pound bay scallops, or sea
scallops halved or
quartered to the size of bay
scallops

1. In a large saucepan of boiling salted water, cook the noodles until almost tender. Add the snow peas and boil 1 to 2 minutes more, or until the noodles are just tender. Drain in a colander and reserve.

2. While the noodles are cooking, in a large, heavy skillet, melt the butter over moderate heat, add the ginger and scallions and cook, stirring, for 5 minutes.

3. Add the wine, bring to a boil, and add the scallops. Simmer, stirring, until the scallops are barely cooked through, about 2 minutes. Remove from the heat, add the noodles and snow peas, and salt and pepper to taste, and toss well. Serve immediately.

caramelized peppered scallops

This Vietnamese-style dish, with its bittersweet caramelized sugar, hot smoky black pepper and pungent garlic and fish sauce, may sound strange to some, but trust me, it tastes great. Serve with plain rice, Carrot Ribbons with Lemon and Cumin (page 180), and Quick Pickled Green Beans (page 178).

serves 4

1½ pounds sea scallops, halved horizontally into rounds

1 teaspoon coarsely ground black pepper

2 tablespoons vegetable oil

3 tablespoons sugar

1 tablespoon chopped garlic

1 tablespoon Asian fish sauce

1 cup packed cilantro sprigs

Cooked rice as an accompaniment

1. Pat the scallops dry and coat with the pepper.

2. Heat the oil in a heavy skillet over moderately high heat. Add the scallops, sugar, and garlic and cook, stirring, for 3 minutes, or until the scallops are just cooked thorough. With a slotted spoon, transfer the scallops to a plate.

3. Boil the liquid in the skillet until it turns a pale golden caramel (see Note). Add ¼ cup water and the fish sauce, and boil for 2 minutes, or until the liquid is slightly syrupy. Spoon the sauce over the scallops and top with the cilantro. Serve immediately with rice.

Note: If you are using "dry," or "diver" scallops, it may not be necessary to remove the scallops from the skillet. Processed or frozen scallops give off water, which makes it necessary to reduce the liquid in order for it to caramelize.

scallops grilled with lemon, garlic, and oregano vinaigrette

Salmoriglio is a Sicilian vinaigrette, made with lemon, garlic, and oregano, that is spooned over seared fish. Here, it is used to baste scallops as they grill, as well as a room-temperature sauce served separately. On the side, try Grapefruit Rice with Chives (page 171), Celery and Lima Bean Puree (page 173), or Sliced Asparagus and Edamame with Olive Oil (page 176).

serves 4

3 tablespoons fresh lemon
juice

2 garlic cloves, minced or
forced through a garlic
press

1 tablespoon fresh oregano
or 1 teaspoon dried
oregano

½ teaspoon salt

¼ teaspoon black pepper

5 tablespoons extra virgin
olive oil

1½ pounds large sea
scallops (see Note)

1. In a small bowl, whisk together the lemon juice, garlic, oregano, salt, and pepper. Add the oil in a stream, whisking until it is emulsified.

2. In a large bowl toss the scallops with half the sauce, and let marinate for 30 minutes. Thread the scallops onto metal skewers. (Bamboo skewers can be used in place of metal ones, but they must be soaked in warm water for at least 1 hour to keep them from catching fire.)

3. Grill the scallops on a hot preheated grill, brushing with any extra marinade remaining in the bowl, until cooked through, about 4 minutes on each side.

4. Serve the scallops immediately with the remaining sauce.

Note: When skewering scallops it is best to use "dry" scallops. They are firmer than "wet" or "soaked" scallops, and are less likely to stick to the grill and pull through the skewer (see page 54).

broiled scallops wrapped in basil and bacon with orange balsamic vinegar

Crisp bacon surrounding aromatic basil and soft sweet scallops, topped with an intense reduction of balsamic vinegar and orange juice—sounds fancy, but it is easy to prepare. If you want to dress it down, serve wedges of lemon on the side in place of the sauce. Side dishes can include Roasted Maple Butter Acorn Squash (page 177), Eggless Caesar Salad (page 188), and Two Potato Hash (page 170).

serves 4

About 40 large basil leaves,
   rinsed and spun dry
2 pounds large sea scallops
   (about 20)
About 10 slices bacon, cut in
   half crosswise

for the sauce

½ cup orange juice
⅓ cup balsamic vinegar
½ teaspoon black pepper

1. Wrap 2 basil leaves in a band around each scallop, wrap a half slice of bacon over the basil, and thread onto a metal skewer, securing the bacon. (Bamboo skewers can be used in place of metal ones, but they must be soaked in warm water for at least 1 hour to keep them from catching fire.) Continue wrapping the scallops and threading them onto skewers, leaving a small space between each, and refrigerate until ready to cook.

2. In a medium saucepan, boil the orange juice and vinegar until the mixture is reduced to about ⅓ cup, reducing the heat near the end so as not to scorch the syrup. Stir in the pepper.

3. Preheat the broiler with a rack set in the uppermost position. Arrange the skewers on a rack set in a shallow baking pan, and broil for 5 minutes on each side, or until the bacon is crisp and the scallops are just firm.

4. Immediately serve the scallops, drizzled lightly with the orange balsamic sauce. Serve any remaining sauce on the side.

Note: The skewers can be grilled rather than broiled. Preheat the grill and brush or wipe it with vegetable oil to keep the skewers from sticking. The cooking time is about the same.

curried coconut scallops

This is a great company dish because everything can be prepared in advance, leaving only the broiling for the last minute. Serve over Grapefruit Rice with Chives (page 171), along with Carrot Ribbons with Lemon and Cumin (page 180) or Green Salad with Grapes and Sunflower Seeds (page 187).

serves 4

½ cup coarsely chopped scallions (a.k.a. green onions)

3 tablespoons chopped peeled fresh ginger (about a 1-inch chunk)

1 garlic clove

1 jalapeño chile, stemmed

2 teaspoons curry powder

¾ teaspoon salt

½ cup unsweetened coconut milk (stir well before measuring)

2 pounds sea scallops

1. In a blender or food processor, combine the scallions, ginger, garlic, jalapeño (including the seeds), curry powder, and salt, and blend into a paste. Add the coconut milk and puree until almost smooth, scraping down the sides of the container often.

2. Pat the scallops dry and arrange them in a flameproof casserole or skillet just large enough to hold them in a single layer. Drizzle the curry sauce on top, coating the scallops well.

The scallops can be prepared up to this point 4 hours in advance, covered, and refrigerated.

3. Preheat the broiler with a rack set 6 inches from the heat. Broil the scallops for 8 to 10 minutes, or until browned and just cooked through. Serve immediately.

Note: Because the scallops are insulated in the sauce, the only way to tell if they are cooked through is to cut one open.

scallops in tahini sauce
with parsley and pine nuts

Ever since my mother-in-law made me tuna fish with tahini, pine nuts, fried onions, and parsley, a recipe her Lebanese neighbor taught her, I have been addicted to the flavors. Here, the nutty, creamy tahini blankets scallops, while the lemon and fresh parsley cut the richness. This main course calls for bright and refreshing side dishes, such as Carrot Ribbons with Lemon and Cumin (page 180), Sprouts and Sliced Tomato Salad (page 179), or Carolina Vinegar Slaw (page 182).

serves 4

3 tablespoons tahini (sesame paste), stir well before measuring

2 tablespoons fresh lemon juice

2 tablespoons extra virgin olive oil

¼ cup pine nuts

1½ pounds sea scallops, patted dry

1 cup coarsely chopped fresh parsley, preferably Italian or flat-leaf

1. In a small bowl, whisk together the tahini, lemon juice, and 2 tablespoons water until creamy. Set aside.

2. In a large, heavy skillet, heat the oil over moderate heat. Add the pine nuts and cook, stirring constantly, until the nuts are golden brown, but do not let them burn. With a slotted spoon, transfer the nuts to a dish.

3. Season the scallops with salt and pepper and add them to the skillet. Cook the scallops over moderate heat for 3 to 5 minutes on each side, or until just cooked through, and transfer them to a plate. Add the tahini sauce to the skillet, whisking until smooth, and return the scallops, stirring to coat them with the sauce. Serve the scallops immediately, topped with the pine nuts and parsley.

Note: This dish is delicious as it is, but if you really want the full flavor combination, fry sliced onions in oil until golden brown (they can be kept warm in the oven) and sprinkle them over each serving.

seared scallops in gazpacho

*T*his *is a great dish for summer entertaining. The gazpacho makes use of a number of fresh summer vegetables and can be made up to a day ahead, leaving only the scallops to cook at the last minute. The scallops are also delicious grilled and placed atop the cool vegetable soup, which acts as a sauce, salad, and vegetable, leaving only bread as an obvious accompaniment.*

**serves 4 as a main course
or 6 as an appetizer**

1 large ripe tomato, diced
(about 1½ cups)

½ yellow bell pepper, seeded
and diced (about ½ cup)

1 small cucumber, peeled and
diced (about ¾ cup)

½ cup diced sweet onions,
such as Vidalia

1 garlic clove, minced

¼ cup packed fresh parsley
leaves

¼ cup plus 1 tablespoon
olive oil

2 tablespoons fresh lemon or
lime juice

½ cup bottled clam juice,
chicken broth, or shell
stock (see page 4)

1½ pounds sea scallops

1. In a blender or food processor, combine the tomato, bell pepper, cucumber, onion, garlic, parsley, the ¼ cup oil, lemon juice, and clam juice. Pulse the motor until the ingredients are finely chopped and soupy. Transfer the gazpacho to a bowl, season with salt and pepper, and refrigerate, covered, at least 2 hours and up to 24.

2. Just before serving, pat the scallops dry and season with salt and pepper. In a large nonstick skillet, heat the remaining 1 tablespoon oil over moderate heat until hot. Add the scallops, in batches if necessary to allow space around each, and cook for 3 to 5 minutes on each side, or until they are just cooked through.

3. Spoon the gazpacho into shallow bowls and top with the hot scallops. Serve immediately.

silky scallop and tofu chowder

Stop! Wait! *Don't just skip this page because you don't understand or like tofu. Soft tofu provides the perfect light but creamy base for this delicious chowder without excess fat and cholesterol. If you are trying to incorporate healthful soybean products into your diet, you'll love it, and if you think you don't like tofu, try this soup and surprise yourself.*

makes about 4¼ cups; serves 2 to 4

1 small onion, chopped
  (about 1 cup)

2 tablespoons vegetable or
  olive oil

1½ tablespoons all-purpose
  flour

2 cups bottled clam juice or
  shell stock (see page 4)

One 12-ounce package soft
  tofu (about 1½ cups)

¾ cup frozen peas

¾ pound bay scallops or sea
  scallops, cut into ½-inch
  pieces

2 tablespoons chopped fresh
  dill

1. In a large, heavy saucepan, cook the onion in the oil over medium heat, stirring, until softened, about 10 minutes. Add the flour and cook, stirring, 1 minute. Stir in the clam juice and simmer for 2 minutes.

2. Pour the soup into a blender or food processor, add the tofu, and puree until completely smooth. Return the mixture to the saucepan and add the peas.

The soup can be made up to this point 8 hours in advance, covered, and refrigerated.

3. Bring the soup to a gentle simmer and add the scallops. Bring the soup back to a simmer, and stir in the dill and salt and pepper to taste. (The scallops will be cooked through when the soup reaches a simmer.)

Note: Tofu comes in many forms, which can be confusing, but there are some standards. Nearly every supermarket now carries tofu packed in shelf-stable, cardboard boxes that do not need to be refrigerated. They are often found in the refrigerator case. It is also sold packed in water in plastic containers or in bulk. Tofu is classified and labeled as soft, firm, and extra firm. Soft, which is called for in this soup, is good for pureeing in sauces and soups. For the creamiest texture, use the tofu in the shelf-stable boxes.

clams and mussels

clams

As with all fish and shellfish, the types of clams available to the home cook vary depending on the region in which she/he lives. Luckily, nearly all clams can be used interchangeably, so the freshest clam is the best choice. Remember, generally the larger the clam, the tougher the muscle, so smaller clams are sought after for eating raw and larger clams are suited for chopping to use in soups, fritters, and stuffings.

atlantic hard-shell clams

Atlantic hard-shell clams, or quahogs (Ko-hogs), are divided into size categories:

Little Necks are the smallest, with shells about 2 inches wide.
Cherrystones are the next size up, with shells up to 3 inches wide.
Chowder clams are the largest.
Small **Mahogany** clams are harvested in deep ocean waters, and
    have reddish-brown shells.

pacific hard-shell clams

Pacific hard-shell clams include:

Littlenecks (not to be confused with the Atlantic Little Necks) are
small, about 1 inch wide, and are often called **Steamers** on the
West Coast.

Manila clams are a longer, flatter version of the littlenecks.

Butter clams are larger, 2 to 5 inches wide, and are similar to
Altlantic hard-shell clams.

The famous giant northwestern **Geoduck** (GOO-ee-duck), with
its elephant trunklike siphon, averages 3 pounds, but can grow to 12
pounds and to 100 years of age. The meat of the siphon is prized
for "giant clam" sushi.

soft-shells and steamers

Another type of clam has a brittle, oval-shaped shell with a long,
dark siphon protruding between the shells from one end. Known in
the Northeast as **Maine steamers**, and in the mid-Atlantic region
and West Coast as **Soft-Shell** or **Long Necks**, these clams are
usually steamed in the shell and served with a dish of hot broth (for
rinsing off any sand) and melted butter for dipping. They are the
preferred type of clam for frying in the East, with bellies or
without (sometimes called "clam strips"). Other soft-shell clams,
Razor and **Jackknife**, have shells shaped like their names (the razor
being the old-fashioned straight-edge type). They are also delicious
steamed or fried.

Very small **Cockles**, which look, taste, and can be cooked like
clams, are not technically in the quahog family. They are appearing
more regularly in American markets, come from New Zealand and
Asia, and can make an intriguing appetizer.

cleaning

Clams should be stored refrigerated, in a bowl, covered with a damp cloth. They can be stored for up to 48 hours, but do not clean them until you are ready to cook. Scrub each clam well under cool running water. Some clams may have slightly gaping shells but should close when squeezed or poked. If they are very cold, they will close very slowly. If not, they may be dead and should be discarded.

mussels

Growing up in Connecticut on Long Island Sound, I was used to seeing long, black-shelled mussels clinging to rocks, docks, and pilings at low tide. My brother and I used to smash them with rocks to expose the beige icky animal inside, but we never would have dreamed of eating them. I now know what I was missing; their briny tender, plump meats are truly delicious. Through cultivation and strict harvesting regulations, mussels are safe to eat, and available year-round. You should not harvest them yourself unless you are sure about the quality of the water in which they live.

live mussels

The most common mussels are the live **Blue** or **common** type, but beautiful **New Zealand Green** or **Green-Lipped** mussels have also become very popular. If buying mussels in a bag, look at the expiration date and get the freshest possible. You can always ask the fish seller if they have fresher bags in storage.

cleaning

Mussels should be kept refrigerated in a bowl, covered with a damp cloth. (If they came in a vented or mesh bag they can stay in it.)

Do not clean mussels until you are ready to cook them, which should be within 48 hours. Scrub each mussel well with a brush, under cool running water, and pull off the hairy beard if visible. While scrubbing, try squeezing and sliding the shells apart. If the mussel is dead or the shells are full of mud, the shells will slide open and you should discard them. With controlled growing, mussels are very clean these days and it has been many years since I have found a mud-filled shell. Also, some mussels may have gaping shells but should close when squeezed or poked. If they are very cold, they will close very slowly. If not, the mussel may be dead and should be discarded.

frozen mussels

Buying frozen green mussels on the half shell can drastically cut preparation time. In addition to their fine quality, they eliminate the need for scrubbing and sorting. The large size is also ideal for broiling and serving in the shell. Cooked, shelled, and frozen mussel meat is also available in many markets (especially Asian markets). This is convenient when the shells are not needed, such as in soups, salads, and for frying.

general serving sizes for steaming:

CLAMS

- 6 to 8 steamed 2-inch hard-shell clams for a first course or 24 for a main course
- ½ pound steamed soft-shell clams for a first course or 1½ to 2 pounds for a main course

MUSSELS

- For steaming use ½ to ¾ pound live or frozen mussels on the half shell, per person, for a first course or 1½ pounds for a main course
- 6 large mussels if stuffed, sauced, or broiled on the half shell for a first course

grilled hard-shell clams with salsa

I *discovered this method of quickly cooking clams to eat out of hand when enjoying freshly opened raw clams at a summer party in 1989. A friend of mine said he liked clams but refused to eat them raw. I asked the clam shucker for a few clams, walked over to the grill, and put them over the fire. Minutes later they popped open, we spooned some salsa on top, and my friend was in heaven.*

Arrange small hard-shell clams (2 inches or smaller) on a preheated grill. With tongs turn them over after about 2 minutes. When the shells open, remove them with tongs to a platter and discard the upper shells. Top with your favorite salsa or cocktail sauce.

Alternatively, you can broil the clams in a shallow baking pan, set very close to the heat.

hard-shell clams or mussels steamed in salsa

It doesn't get easier than this! Some may consider it too easy, or even cheating, so you may want to make it your secret recipe. Just about any bottled salsa provides a perfect base in which to steam briny clams or mussels, and a broth worthy of sopping up with crusty bread. Serve as an appetizer or add Baked Vegetable and Cheese Polenta (page 174), Warm Herbed White Bean Salad (page 172), or Orange Orzo with Basil (page 167) to make it a meal.

**serves 4 as a first course
or 2 as a main course**

1 cup bottled salsa (see Note)

3 pounds live small hard-shell clams or mussels, scrubbed well (see page 73)

1 cup chopped fresh cilantro

In a large pot, bring the salsa and 1 cup water to a boil. Add the clams and cilantro and cover the pot. Steam over high heat, shaking the pot occasionally, for 2 to 8 minutes, or until the shells open. Serve immediately.

Note: I have made this using expensive gourmet salsa and basic store brands with equal results, but I prefer chunky varieties to give texture to the broth. Choose hot, medium, or mild types as desired. Green, tomatillo-based salsas also work well.

steamers with roasted pepper butter

This dipping butter is also delicious for steamed hard-shell clams and mussels. If serving as a main course, serve good bread and Warm Herbed White Bean Salad (page 172), Baked Vegetable and Cheese Polenta (page 174), or Spinach Salad with Blue Cheese and Plum Dressing (page 186).

**serves 4 as a first course
or 2 as a main course**

One 12-ounce jar roasted red
   peppers, drained

1 stick (8 tablespoons) butter

1 tablespoon Worcestershire
   sauce

¼ teaspoon Tabasco or other
   hot sauce, or to taste

2½ pounds live soft-shell
   clams or steamers,
   scrubbed well

1. Pat the peppers dry between sheets of paper towels. In a blender puree the peppers and add to a small saucepan. Add the butter, Worcestershire sauce, and hot sauce, and simmer, stirring, for 2 minutes. Season with salt and pepper and keep warm.

2. In a heavy pot bring 2 inches of water to a boil. Add the clams, cover, and steam for 5 to 7 minutes, or until the shells are open. Transfer the clams to a large serving bowl or individual bowls and pour the broth into cups.

3. Serve the clams with small individual dipping bowls of the cooking broth and pepper butter.

Note: To eat steamers or soft-shell clams, remove the clam from the shell. Peel off the brown membrane covering the "siphon" or "neck." Holding it by the neck, swish it around in the hot broth to rinse off any sand, dip it in sauce or butter, and eat.

linguine with white clam sauce

This classic pasta sauce, with its fresh taste of briny clams and herbs, can be made with any small hard-shell clams. Serve with Eggless Caesar Salad (page 188).

serves 4

4 large garlic cloves, minced

2 tablespoons butter

3 tablespoons olive oil

3 tablespoons all-purpose
  flour

¾ cup dry white wine

2 cups bottled clam juice

1 teaspoon dried thyme or
  2 teaspoons fresh thyme

¾ pound linguine

½ cup chopped fresh parsley

2 pounds live small hard-shell
  clams, scrubbed well

1. In a large, deep skillet, cook the garlic in the butter and oil over moderately low heat, stirring, until it just begins to turn golden. Stir in the flour and cook for 2 minutes. Whisk in the wine, clam juice, and thyme and simmer, whisking occasionally, for 10 minutes.

The sauce can be made up to this point, up to 1 hour in advance. Return to a simmer before continuing.

2. In a large pot of boiling water, cook the linguine until it is tender and drain in a colander.

3. Stir the parsley and clams into the sauce and simmer, covered, for 5 minutes, or until the clams are open. Stir in salt and pepper to taste. Serve the linguine topped with the sauce and clams.

linguine with red clam sauce and pancetta

Versatile clams work equally well with both red and white Italian sauces. This hearty tomato sauce is enriched with pancetta, Italian bacon that is salt cured, not smoked. Enjoy with a bottle of red or white wine, and Eggless Caesar Salad (page 188).

serves 4

1 medium onion, chopped (about 1½ cups)

1 large garlic clove, minced

2 ounces pancetta, cut into ¼-inch dice (about ½ cup)

2 tablespoons olive oil

½ cup dry red wine

One 14.5-ounce can chopped tomatoes with jalapeños, including the juice

¾ pound linguine or spaghetti

2 dozen live small hard-shell clams, scrubbed well

¼ cup chopped fresh parsley

1. In a large, deep skillet, cook the onion, garlic, and pancetta in the oil over moderate heat, stirring, until the vegetables are golden. Add the wine and tomatoes and simmer, stirring occasionally, for 15 minutes.

The sauce can be made up to this point, up to 8 hours in advance, covered, and refrigerated. Bring to a simmer before continuing.

2. In a pot of boiling salted water, cook the linguine until just tender. Drain and rinse briefly.

3. While the pasta is cooking, add the clams to the sauce. Simmer, covered, for 5 minutes, or until the clams open. Add the pasta to the skillet and toss to coat well. Serve with the clams arranged around the edge of each dish, and sprinkle with the parsley.

clams in miso broth with noodles

Miso adds an earthy, salty richness to this light broth, while the ginger peppers it up a bit. Do not add salt to the broth, as the miso and clams do that for you. For a satisfying but light supper, serve with a simple green salad or Quick Pickled Green Beans (page 178).

serves 4 as a main course
or 6 as an appetizer

1 cup thinly sliced scallions (a.k.a. green onions), white and green parts

¼ cup minced peeled fresh ginger

3 tablespoons shiro miso paste (see Note)

1 tablespoon sugar

½ pound thin Japanese soba noodles or spaghetti

3 pounds live small hard-shell clams, scrubbed well

1. In a large pot, simmer 2 cups water with the scallions and ginger for 5 minutes. Add the miso paste and sugar, and whisk until smooth.

The broth can be made up to 2 hours ahead of time and kept at room temperature.

2. Boil the noodles in a pot of salted water just until tender. Drain and rinse.

3. Bring the miso broth to a boil, add the clams, and steam, covered, over high heat, shaking the pot occasionally for 2 to 4 minutes, or until the shells open. Divide the noodles among bowls and spoon the clams and broth on top.

Note: Shiro miso paste, or sweet white miso, looks like peanut butter or a little lighter in color. It is available at Japanese or Asian markets, specialty markets, health-food stores, and some supermarkets. There are a number of different brands of miso (fermented soybean paste), packaged in plastic bags or plastic tubs. The easiest way to identify this mild type is by its color. Brown and red misos are much stronger in flavor. Miso can be kept covered and refrigerated for months. (Eventually, the flavor dissipates but it does not go rancid.)

a hat trick of clam chowders

The southwest end of Connecticut, the part of New England where I grew up, is just over the border from New York City and the island of Manhattan. Though geographically close, New England and Manhattan clam chowders couldn't be further apart. This has resulted in my own soup identity crisis. My parents look at the creamy version (New England) with a little disdain—too fattening—not pure enough. They prefer the cleaner, more sophisticated, tomato version (Manhattan). I enjoy both, but being a bit rebellious I have to admit that spooning into a bowl of slightly decadent creamy white clammy chowder is one of life's finest pleasures.

There is even a third, broth-based clam chowder, from Rhode Island, which I am sure has caused even more family disagreements throughout the Northeast. It is basically New England clam chowder without the cream.

All three versions have a distinct briny clam flavor.

new england clam chowder

3 dozen 2½- to 3-inch live
   hard-shell clams, scrubbed
   well (6 to 7 pounds)

2 cups bottled clam juice

1 medium onion, chopped
   (about 1½ cups)

½ stick (4 tablespoons) butter

2 tablespoons all-purpose
   flour

1½ cups chopped celery

2 medium red boiling
   potatoes, diced

¼ teaspoon dried thyme

1 bay leaf

2 cups half-and-half

1. In a large pot, combine the clams and 1 cup of the clam juice. Bring the liquid to a boil and cook, covered, shaking the pot occasionally and removing the clams as they open. Discard any clams that have not opened after 10 minutes.

2. Discard the shells, coarsely chop the clams, and set aside. Strain the clam broth through a fine sieve into a bowl and rinse out the pot.

3. In the pot, cook the onion in the butter over moderate heat, stirring, until softened. Stir in the flour and cook for 1 minute. Pour in the reserved broth, letting any sand remain in the bottom of the bowl, and add the remaining clam juice, the clams, celery, potatoes, thyme, and bay leaf. Simmer, uncovered, for 25 minutes.

4. Stir in the half-and-half and salt and pepper to taste. Bring to a boil, remove the bay leaf, and serve.

The chowder can be made 1 day in advance, covered, and refrigerated, or it can be frozen for up to 6 months.

manhattan clam chowder

makes about 7 cups

3 dozen 2½- to 3-inch live
   hard-shell clams, scrubbed
   well (6 to 7 pounds)

2 cups bottled clam juice

1 medium onion, chopped
   (about 1½ cups)

2 garlic cloves, minced

3 tablespoons olive oil

1½ cups chopped celery

One 28-ounce can crushed
   tomatoes

½ teaspoon dried thyme

½ teaspoon dried oregano

½ teaspoon fennel seeds

1 bay leaf

Freshly ground black pepper

1. In a large pot, combine the clams and 1 cup of the clam juice. Bring the liquid to a boil and cook, covered, shaking the pot occasionally and removing the clams as they open. Discard any clams that have not opened after 10 minutes.

2. Discard the shells, coarsely chop the clams, and set aside. Strain the clam broth through a fine sieve into a bowl and rinse out the pot.

3. In the pot, cook the onion and garlic in the oil over moderate heat, stirring, until softened. Add the reserved clam broth, letting any sand remain in the bottom of the bowl, and add the remaining clam juice, the clams, celery, tomatoes, thyme, oregano, fennel seeds, and bay leaf. Simmer, partially covered, for 30 minutes. Remove the bay leaf.

4. Add pepper to taste and serve.

The chowder can be made 1 day in advance, covered, and refrigerated, or it can be frozen for up to 6 months.

rhode island clam chowder

makes about 6 cups

3 dozen 2½- to 3-inch live
   hard-shell clams, scrubbed
   well (6 to 7 pounds)

3 slices bacon, cut crosswise
   into ¼-inch-wide strips

2 tablespoons olive oil

1 medium onion, chopped
   (about 1½ cups)

1 cup chopped celery

2 cups bottled clam juice

1 pound all-purpose potatoes
   (about 2 medium), peeled
   and diced (about 1½ cups)

1 bay leaf

2 tablespoon fresh minced
   dill or 1 teaspoon dried dill

2 tablespoons minced fresh
   parsley

1. In a large pot, combine the clams and 2 cups water. Bring the liquid to a boil and cook, covered, stirring occasionally and removing the clams as they open. Discard any clams that have not opened after 10 minutes.

2. Discard the shells, coarsely chop the clams, and set aside. Strain the clam broth through a fine sieve into a bowl and rinse out the pot.

3. In the pot, cook the bacon over moderate heat, stirring, until it is browned, and, with a slotted spoon, transfer it to a dish.

4. Pour off the fat and add the oil, onion, and celery. Cook, stirring, over moderate heat for 2 minutes. Add the reserved clam broth, letting any sand remain in the bottom of the bowl, and add the clam juice, potatoes, and bay leaf. Simmer, partially covered, for 10 minutes, or until the potatoes are tender. Add the clams, dill, parsley, and salt and pepper to taste. Remove the bay leaf.

The chowder can be made 1 day in advance, covered, and refrigerated, or it can be frozen for up to 6 months.

mussels or clams steamed with fennel and vermouth

This is a delicate way to serve steamed mussels or clams. Use one of the mussel shells as a spoon to scoop out the other mussels and drink the broth. Serve with Baked Vegetable and Cheese Polenta (page 174) and Green Salad with Grapes and Sunflower Seeds (page 187).

serves 4 as a first course
or 2 as a main course

½ cup thinly sliced shallots
   or red onions

1 small fennel bulb, thinly
   sliced

½ teaspoon fennel seeds

2 large garlic cloves, chopped

¼ cup olive oil

1 cup vermouth

1 teaspoon dried thyme

3 pounds live small hard-shell
   mussels or clams,
   scrubbed well (see
   page 73)

1. In a large, deep skillet or pot, cook the shallot, sliced fennel, fennel seeds, and garlic in the oil over moderate heat until softened, about 5 minutes. Add the vermouth and thyme and boil for 2 minutes. Add the mussels and increase the heat to moderately high. Cover and cook the mussels for 2 to 10 minutes, shaking the pan occasionally, until the mussels open.

2. Spoon the mussels into bowls and ladle the broth and vegetables on top.

broiled mussels or clams with caesar mayonnaise

The distinctive flavors of Caesar salad—garlic, anchovy, mustard, and Parmesan—are combined with mayonnaise and bread crumbs to form a creamy, crusty topping for clams or mussels. For an all-Caesar experience, mound Eggless Caesar Salad (page 188) on salad plates and arrange the hot mussels or clams around the rims.

makes 12; serves 4 as an appetizer

12 large live mussels or small hard-shell clams (2 inches wide), scrubbed well (see page 73)

2 tablespoons mayonnaise

½ teaspoon anchovy paste

1 teaspoon fresh lemon juice plus lemon wedges as an accompaniment

1 teaspoon Dijon mustard

¼ teaspoon minced garlic

¼ teaspoon freshly ground black pepper

¼ cup freshly grated Parmesan

2 tablespoons fresh or dried bread crumbs

1. Preheat the broiler with a rack set in the top third and bottom third of the oven.

2. Arrange the mussels in a shallow baking pan. Broil on the top rack for 2 to 3 minutes, or until the shells just open.

3. In a small bowl, whisk together the mayonnaise, anchovy paste, lemon juice, mustard, garlic, and black pepper. Stir in the Parmesan and bread crumbs.

4. Break off and discard one of the shells from each clam or mussel. Top each with about 1 teaspoon of the Caesar paste, spreading to cover the shellfish, and arrange them in the baking pan. Broil on the lower rack of the oven for 3 to 5 minutes, or until the tops are golden. Serve immediately with lemon wedges.

mussels with smoked sausage and kale

This Portuguese-inspired combination of shellfish, meat, and kale cannot truly be enjoyed without some good bread (or broa*) to soak up the broth. Plain boiled potatoes, Roasted Maple Butter Acorn Squash (page 177), or Two Potato Hash (page 170) are welcome alongside this hearty fare.*

serves 4

½ pound (½ ring) kielbasa, diced (about 1½ cups)

1 large onion, coarsely chopped

2 tablespoons olive oil

¼ to ½ teaspoon hot red pepper flakes

¼ pound fresh kale, washed, coarse stems discarded, and leaves chopped (about 2 packed cups)

3 pounds live mussels, scrubbed well (see page 73), or frozen on the half shell

1. In a large saucepan, cook the kielbasa and onion in the oil over moderate heat, stirring occasionally, until the onion begins to brown, about 15 minutes. Add the pepper flakes, 1 cup water, and kale and simmer, covered, for 5 minutes.

This mixture can be made up to 1 hour in advance, reserved, off the heat, uncovered.

2. Bring the kale mixture to a boil, add the mussels, and cook, covered, stirring occasionally, until the shells open (about 5 minutes for frozen mussels). Discard any unopened mussels. Serve immediately in bowls.

Note: Kale is a hearty but mild green that keeps its texture and brilliant color after cooking. Other greens can be substituted, such as spinach, collards, beet greens, cabbage, and chard.

mussels steamed in carrot-ginger broth

This dish looks as bright as it tastes, with its black- or green-lipped mussel shells, sitting in a shocking orange sauce. To complement the refreshing taste of ginger and lime, serve it with Potato Salad with Roasted Peppers and Sesame Seeds (page 169), Jollof Rice (page 168), or Celery and Lima Bean Puree (page 173), and a tossed salad, such as Green Salad with Grapes and Sunflower Seeds (page 187).

serves 4 as a first course
or 2 as a main course

1 large garlic clove, chopped

2 tablespoons butter

1 cup carrot juice

2 tablespoons minced peeled
fresh ginger

½ cup thinly sliced scallions
(a.k.a. green onions)

2 tablespoons fresh lime juice

3 pounds live mussels,
scrubbed well (see
page 73), or frozen on the
half shell

1. In a large pot, cook the garlic in the butter over moderate heat, stirring, until pale golden. Add the carrot juice and ginger, and boil the liquid until reduced by half.

2. Add the scallions, lime juice, and mussels, and steam, covered, over moderately high heat, shaking the pot occasionally, for 5 to 10 minutes, or until the shells open (or until the mussels on the half shell are heated through). Discard any unopened mussels and serve immediately.

Note: The mussels can also be served chilled on the half shell. After steaming, arrange the mussels on a platter, each in one of its shells. Spoon the broth over them and refrigerate, covered, for 1 hour. They can be made in advance and chilled for up to 12 hours.

mussels in green chile sauce

A classic Mexican green chile sauce is made by pureeing tomatillos, chiles, onion, and garlic. When heated and simmered with mussels, it serves as a spicy but light sauce, delicious slurped up with the briny shellfish. To make a meal, serve Orange Orzo with Basil (page 167) or Jollof Rice (page 168), Summer Corn on the Cob with Basil Butter (page 175), and Green Salad with Grapes and Sunflower Seeds (page 187).

serves 4 as a first course
or 2 as a main course

2 fresh jalapeño chiles

1 pound fresh tomatillos, coarsely chopped, or canned tomatillo puree (see Note)

½ cup dry white wine

½ cup chopped onions

2 large garlic cloves, minced

¼ cup olive oil

2 teaspoons sugar

1 teaspoon dried oregano

3 pounds live mussels, scrubbed well (see page 73), or frozen on the half shell

½ cup chopped fresh cilantro

1. In a blender, puree the jalapeños, tomatillos, and wine.

2. In a large, heavy pot, cook the onion and garlic in the oil until softened and add the tomatillo mixture, sugar, and oregano. Add the mussels and steam for 5 to 8 minutes, stirring occasionally, until the shells open (or the frozen mussels are heated through). Stir in the cilantro and serve immediately.

Note: Tomatillos are vegetables that look like small green tomatoes, surrounded by a loose papery shell. They are widely available in supermarkets, usually near the avocados and tomatoes. If you cannot find them, ask your produce manager. If they know someone wants them, they might order them.

Discard the papery shell and chop the vegetable without coring it. Add the fresh, zesty, slightly acidic vegetable to stews, sauces, and dips.

mussels in parsley sauce

The shocking-green sauce is full of fresh herb flavor and is as simple as can be. Always serve this dish with bread, and for a main course, add Two Potato Hash (page 170) or Orange Orzo with Basil (page 167).

serves 4 as a first course
or 2 as a main course

3 cups packed fresh parsley
leaves

6 tablespoons olive oil

3 tablespoons medium-dry
sherry

¾ teaspoon salt

¼ teaspoon black pepper

2 large garlic cloves, minced

2 pounds live mussels,
scrubbed well (see
page 73), or frozen on the
half shell

1. In a blender, puree the parsley with 4 tablespoons of the oil, the sherry, salt, and pepper.

2. In a large, heavy pot, heat the remaining 2 tablespoons oil over moderately high heat; add the garlic and cook, stirring, for 30 seconds until it starts to color. Add the mussels and parsley sauce and cook, tossing the mussels, for 5 minutes, or until the shells open. Discard any unopened mussels and serve immediately.

linguine with mussels in vodka tomato sauce

According to New York radio foodie Arthur Schwartz, the idea for tomato, vodka, and cream sauce came out of a contest for chefs in Italy, sponsored by a company promoting chile-flavored vodka in the mid- to late 1970s. Since then tomato and vodka sauce has become an American classic. Here, the addition of mussels contributes a briny taste. Serve lots of napkins with this dish, since there is no way to eat the mussels without using your hands. Provide a bowl in the center of the table for the shells and dig in. Crusty garlic bread and Eggless Caesar Salad (page 188) are all you need for a meal.

serves 4

1 medium onion, chopped (about 1½ cups)

3 garlic cloves, minced

2 tablespoons olive oil

⅓ cup vodka

One 28-ounce can whole tomatoes, drained

¼ teaspoon hot red pepper flakes

½ teaspoon dried thyme or 1½ teaspoons chopped fresh thyme

½ teaspoon dried basil or 2 tablespoons chopped fresh basil

¾ pound linguine

½ cup heavy cream

2 pounds live mussels, scrubbed well (see page 73), or frozen on the half shell

1. In a large, deep skillet cook the onion and garlic in the oil over moderate heat, stirring, until softened. Add the vodka, tomatoes (breaking them up), pepper flakes, thyme, and basil and simmer 20 minutes, stirring occasionally.

2. In a pot of boiling salted water, cook the linguine until just tender and drain.

3. While the pasta is cooking, add the cream to the skillet. Bring to a boil and add the mussels. Simmer the mussels, covered, stirring occasionally, until they open, and season with salt and pepper. Divide the linguine among plates and top with the mussels and sauce.

mussel, pepper, and leek chowder

This rosy-colored chowder is chock-full of vegetables and plump mussels. Yellow bell peppers can be substituted, but green peppers do not have the same sweetness. Serve as an impressive first course, or add Spinach Salad with Blue Cheese and Plum Dressing (page 186) and some good bread to make a satisfying supper. Any leftovers freeze well.

makes about 10 cups;
serves 6

3 medium leeks, washed well
(see Note) and thinly sliced

3 red bell peppers, seeded
and diced

4 garlic cloves, minced or
pressed in a garlic press

2 celery ribs, chopped

1 bay leaf

3 tablespoons butter

3 pounds live mussels,
scrubbed well (see
page 73), or frozen on the
half shell

4 small red potatoes (1 to
1¼ pounds), scrubbed and
cut into ½-inch dice

2 cups bottled clam juice

1 teaspoon dried basil or
¼ cup chopped fresh basil

1 cup heavy cream

1. In a large, heavy pot, cook the leeks, bell peppers, garlic, celery, and bay leaf in the butter over moderate heat, stirring, for 15 minutes.

2. Meanwhile, bring 1 cup water to a boil in a large, deep skillet. Add the mussels and cook, covered, shaking the pan for 10 minutes, until the shells open (or until the mussels on the half shell are heated through). Remove the mussels, discarding the shells, and coarsely chop the mussels. Strain the cooking liquid through a fine sieve into a measuring cup. Add enough water to make 1½ cups broth or boil it until it is reduced to 1½ cups.

3. To the leeks add the mussel broth, potatoes, clam juice, and basil, and simmer for 15 minutes.

4. Discard the bay leaf. Transfer 2 cups of the chowder to a blender or food processor and puree until smooth. Stir the puree, chopped mussels, and cream into the chowder and season with salt and pepper.

The soup can be made 1 day ahead, covered and refrigerated, or frozen for up to 6 months.

Note: To clean leeks, trim the root ends and tough green leaves. Split each leek lengthwise, leaving it attached at the root end, and rub the grit out of each layer, holding the leek upside down under running water.

Coppery, sweet, salty, creamy, buttery, briny, tinny, crisp, fruity. These are some of the words used to describe the astounding taste of oysters. Some will only eat them steamed or fried, while other "purists" feel it is a sin to eat them any other way than raw and ice cold.

The first seafood to be cultivated by man was the oyster, in 110 B.C. At times in history they were so plentiful, they were considered peasant food, but today they are a delicacy, usually saved for special occasions. However, containers of preshucked oysters make it easy to add them to a soup or pasta anytime.

seasons

Are oysters a winter-only food? No. There is nothing wrong with oysters in the summer months or months with an "r," but this is the time when they spawn, leaving them in a slightly less prime, plump, succulent state.

oyster liquor

Oyster liquor is not an alcohol; it is the natural juice that surrounds an oyster in its shell. It is often reserved to use in a recipe.

Oysters are cultivated in Atlantic and Pacific waters, from Nova Scotia to the Gulf of Mexico, California to British Columbia. There are dozens of different oysters, ranging in size and taste. The most common oysters are **Bluepoints**, **Wellfleets**, and **Prince Edward** oysters from the East Coast (bluepoints were originally harvested in the Great South Bay on Long Island, New York, but are now cultivated all along the East Coast). **Apalachicolas** are from the Florida Gulf; **Olympias** and **Kumamotos** are from the West Coast. Get to know your local oyster by talking to your local fish dealer. Ask which type he carries, which he prefers, and where they are from. You can read about the different tastes in oysters, but as with wines, there is no way to figure out your own preferences until you taste them. Restaurants that offer a sampling of different oysters are the best places to learn. Comparing oysters side by side makes their differences clear.

Gold Band oysters are Louisiana oysters that have been processed in the shell using HPP (High Pressure Process) to release the oyster from the shell and kill bacteria. Before processing, the oysters are sealed with a wide yellow band, which keeps the oyster closed tightly and the juices inside. To serve, the band is removed and the raw oyster opens easily. Many of the shucked oysters sold in bulk are processed this way.

on the half shell

If you want to enjoy oysters raw, on the half shell, make sure they are legally harvested and bought from a reputable fish seller. Some markets will open the oysters for you and give you the shells in which to serve them. Pasteurized bottled oysters or preshucked oysters sold in bulk are not meant to be eaten raw.

Live oysters are opened with a special knife, which is wedged into the narrow hinge end. It takes practice and can be dangerous if you don't know what you are doing. To help his customers enjoy freshly shucked oysters at home, my local seafood dealer, John Anagnos of City Fish Market, in Wethersfield, Connecticut, developed this easy opening method:

1. Starting with fresh oysters, which have been well chilled on ice, hold the oyster flat with the rounded shell side down.
2. Use a pair of nipper pliers to break off a piece of the brittle thin end of the oyster to expose an opening to the inside.
3. Insert an oyster knife inside the oyster, running it along the top of the shell to cut the muscle, and remove the top shell.
4. Holding the oyster level to retain the juices, slide the knife under the oyster meat to release the muscle from the shell.

sauces for oysters on the half shell

The most common accompaniments for raw oysters are plain lemon or cocktail sauce (basically ketchup and horseradish, which covers up the taste of the oyster). Below are some sauces that complement the taste of oysters rather than overwhelm them. They can be served with raw, steamed, or roasted oysters. To help oyster shells stay level when served, arrange them on a bed of shredded green or purple cabbage or lettuce.

Sour Cream Dill Sauce (page 102)
Pickled Ginger and Sake (step 1, page 103)
Classic Mignonette Sauce (recipe follows)
Artichoke Heart Sauce (recipe follows)
Carrot and Tarragon Sauce (recipe follows)

classic mignonette sauce

This is a classic accompaniment to oysters and gets its name from the French term meaning crushed white pepper.

¼ cup minced shallots

⅓ cup red or white wine
   vinegar

1 teaspoon coarsely ground
   black or white pepper

Stir together all the ingredients and refrigerate, covered, for at least 2 hours.

The sauce keeps for up to 1 week.

artichoke heart sauce

Pureed artichokes make a creamy sauce that looks like mayonnaise but is quite acidic.

½ cup chopped canned
  artichoke hearts (2 to
  3 small)
¼ cup white wine vinegar
2 teaspoons Dijon mustard
1 tablespoon olive oil
¼ teaspoon freshly ground
  black pepper

In a blender, combine all the ingredients and blend until smooth.

The sauce keeps for up to 1 week, covered and refrigerated.

carrot and tarragon sauce

Be sure to use unseasoned rice vinegar because the "seasoned" kind is too sweet and salty for this sauce.

makes about ½ cup

¼ cup finely grated carrots
(use the small round holes
of a grater)

⅓ cup unseasoned rice
vinegar

1 teaspoon minced fresh
tarragon

Stir together all the ingredients. Cover and refrigerate for at least 1 hour.

The sauce keeps for up to 3 days, covered and refrigerated.

grilled or "roasted" oysters

Native Americans cooked oysters this way, and I bet the Romans liked this cooking method as well when they began cultivating oysters in 110 B.C. A hot fire, cold beer, and melted butter are the only ingredients necessary for a perfect oyster roast. (Oven mitts or kitchen towels help to handle the hot shells.)

2 dozen fresh oysters in their
    shells, scrubbed well

½ stick (4 tablespoons)
    butter, melted

Lemon wedges, hot sauce, or
    horseradish as
    accompaniments (optional)

serves 8 to 12 as a first course

Over glowing coals or a preheated gas grill, arrange the oysters, rounded shell side down. Cover the grill and let them roast for 1 to 2 minutes. Remove the oysters as they open, even slightly. Continue to cook for up to 8 minutes until all shells have opened. Serve with butter and, if desired, lemon wedges, hot sauce, or horseradish.

Note: Oyster shells do not always pop wide open like clam shells. Force a knife between the gaping shells and pry apart to extract meat.

chilled steamed oysters in sour cream dill sauce

This simple hors d'oeuvre may convert even the most skeptical eaters. I love the combination of oysters and dill, and sour cream adds just the right amount of richness.

serves 4 as an appetizer

1 pint shucked oysters (about 16), including their liquor, checked for shell fragments

½ cup sour cream

2 tablespoons Dijon mustard

2 tablespoons wine vinegar or fresh lemon juice

1 teaspoon sugar

¼ teaspoon salt

¼ teaspoon black pepper

3 tablespoon chopped fresh dill

1. Put the oysters with their liquor in a small, heavy saucepan and heat over moderately high heat just until their edges curl. Transfer to a bowl and add a few ice cubes to stop the oysters from cooking. Chill, covered, until cold, about 1½ hours.

2. In a small bowl, whisk together the sour cream, mustard, vinegar, sugar, salt, and pepper. Stir in the dill. Drain the oysters and gently stir into the sauce. Serve cold with crackers, or on a bed of lettuce as an appetizer.

Note: For a formal hors d'oeuvre, spoon the oysters into endive slices, small lettuce leaves, or cleaned oyster shells.

oysters baked on the half shell with sake and pickled ginger

The intense but clean tastes of sake and ginger with salty, earthy miso create a sauce that mimics the complex taste of oysters.

1 cup sake (Japanese rice wine)

1 tablespoon pickled ginger slices (the type served with sushi, natural or pink color), cut into slivers

1 teaspoon sweet white miso paste (a.k.a. shiro miso or *Saikyo*)

1 dozen fresh oysters in the shell, scrubbed well

1. In a small saucepan, boil the sake with the ginger until it is reduced to ¼ cup. Stir in the miso and reserve.

2. Preheat a broiler with a rack set in the upper third of the oven. Arrange the oysters in a shallow baking pan, rounded shell side down. Broil the oysters for 1 to 3 minutes, or until the shells open slightly, releasing some juices. Using a towel to hold each hot oyster, carefully pry the shells apart with a knife, discarding the top shell.

3. Arrange the oysters on the half shell on a platter and drizzle each with some of the sauce. Serve immediately or chill, covered, for up to 1 hour. The oysters can be served warm or chilled.

Note: Shiro miso paste, or sweet white miso, is the color of peanut butter or sometimes a little lighter. It is available at Japanese or Asian markets, specialty markets, health-food stores, and some supermarkets. There are a number of different brands of miso (fermented soybean paste), packaged in plastic bags or plastic tubs. The easiest way to identify this mild type is by its color. Brown and red misos are much stronger in flavor. Miso can be kept, covered and refrigerated, for months. Eventually the flavor dissipates, but it does not go rancid.

oysters roasted in mushroom caps
with garlic butter and parsley

With the briny saltiness of the oyster and the meaty smoothness of the mushrooms, these delicacies taste very similar to escargots. They could certainly be cooked in and served on an escargot plate as an appetizer, with bread, of course, to sop up the garlic butter.

makes 24 hors d'oeuvres

½ stick (4 tablespoons)
   butter, softened

1½ teaspoons minced garlic

2 tablespoons minced fresh
   parsley

24 mushrooms (about
   2 inches wide), wiped clean
   and stems discarded

24 shucked oysters (about
   24 ounces), drained and
   checked for shell fragments

½ lemon

1. Preheat the oven to 400°F.

2. In a small bowl, mash together the butter, garlic, and parsley with a fork. Arrange the mushroom caps in a shallow baking pan, stemmed end up, and top with half the butter mixture (about ½ teaspoon in each cap).

3. Bake for 15 minutes. Put an oyster in each cap, top with the remaining butter, and bake 10 minutes more. Sprinkle the caps with lemon juice and salt and pepper to taste.

fresh and smoked oysters under broiled caper and scallion cream

The surprise in these hot broiled creamy oysters is the smoked oyster tucked under each fresh one, adding a deep earthy flavor.

makes 12 hors d'oeuvres

2 tablespoons cream cheese

¼ cup mayonnaise

2 tablespoons drained capers

2 tablespoons minced
scallions (a.k.a. green
onions)

1 tablespoon minced fresh
parsley

1 teaspoon fresh lemon juice

1 dozen fresh oysters in the
shell, scrubbed well (see
Note)

12 canned smoked oysters

1. In a small bowl, stir together the cream cheese, mayonnaise, capers, scallions, parsley, lemon juice, and salt and pepper to taste.

2. Preheat a broiler with a rack set in the upper third of the oven. Arrange the oysters in a shallow baking pan, rounded shell side down. Broil the oysters for 1 to 3 minutes, or until the shells open slightly, releasing some juices. Using a towel to hold each hot oyster, carefully pry the shells apart with a knife, discarding the top (flat) shell.

3. Tuck a smoked oyster under each fresh oyster in the shell. Divide the caper cream among the oysters, spreading it to cover the tops, and arrange them in the baking pan. Broil the oysters 6 inches from the heat until the topping is browned, about 5 minutes. Serve immediately.

Note: To avoid opening fresh oysters yourself, or steaming them open in the oven, buy fresh-shucked oysters and ask to keep the shells. Or, for an easy way to open oysters, follow the procedure on page 97. Once you find oyster shells that rest level on a surface and have a nice rounded indentation, keep them and reuse them for broiling and stuffing.

scalloped oysters

For the past few years my parents have joined with friends at their church to celebrate Thanksgiving dinner. People are asked to bring side dishes to accompany the roast turkey, and as a result they are able to experience a little of everyone's holiday tradition. One of their new favorite Thanksgiving dishes, brought by a friend, is scalloped oysters. The old-time term "scalloped" refers to a mixture baked in milk or cream sauce, and scalloped oysters have been served for generations in the United Kingdom and the New England and mid-Atlantic states.

serves 4 to 6

1 cup crushed saltine crackers (about 40 crackers)

½ cup dried bread crumbs

½ stick (4 tablespoons) butter, melted

2 tablespoons minced fresh parsley

1 pint shucked oysters (about 16), including their liquor, checked for shell fragments

¾ cup heavy cream

1½ teaspoons Worcestershire sauce

1. Preheat the oven to 350°F.

2. In a medium bowl, combine the cracker and bread crumbs, butter, parsley, and salt and pepper to taste, and toss until the crumbs are coated with butter. Spread half the mixture in the bottom of a 9-inch round baking dish or pan. Lay the oysters on top, reserving the oyster liquor, and cover with the remaining crumbs.

3. Strain the oyster liquor through a sieve into a bowl to remove any shell pieces. (There should be about ½ cup liquor.) To the bowl add the cream and Worcestershire sauce, and pour the sauce over the crumbs.

4. Bake, uncovered, until puffed and brown, about 45 minutes.

Note: This recipe doubles perfectly when baked in a 9 × 13-inch baking dish.

oyster rockefeller gratin

Creamed oysters and creamed spinach are all baked into one tempting casserole, with a crunchy bread crumb and bacon topping. Serve as an elegant side dish with roast beef or turkey, or prepare in individual ramekins for an impressive first course.

serves 6 as an appetizer
or side dish

4 slices bacon, chopped

1 teaspoon fennel seeds

2 cups fresh bread crumbs

1 cup chopped onions
   (1 small)

2 tablespoons butter

2 tablespoons all-purpose
   flour

1 cup half-and-half

1 pound fresh baby spinach,
   washed and dried

1 pint shucked oysters (about
   16), drained and checked
   for shell fragments

½ teaspoon salt, or to taste

1. Preheat the oven to 400°F.

2. In a medium skillet, cook the bacon and fennel seeds over moderate heat, stirring, until the bacon begins to turn brown. Remove from the heat and stir in the bread crumbs and salt and pepper to taste. Reserve.

3. In a large skillet, cook the onions in the butter over moderate heat, stirring, until softened. Add the flour and cook, stirring, for 2 minutes. Add the half-and-half and bring to a simmer, stirring. Add the spinach and cook, stirring, until the spinach is wilted, about 10 minutes. Remove the skillet from the heat and stir in the oysters and salt and pepper to taste.

4. Transfer the mixture to a 9-inch pie plate and top with the crumb mixture. Bake in the middle of the oven for 20 to 25 minutes, or until browned and bubbling. Let cool for 10 minutes before serving.

oyster and sausage gumbo

Gumbo represents the melting pot of cultures that make up New Orleans and the greater Gulf Coast of Louisiana. African, Spanish, French, and American ingredients and techniques all contribute to this rich, unique stew. Everyone's gumbo is different, and there seem to be no limits as to what can be thrown into the pot. Gumbo is really a whole meal in a bowl, but Quick Pickled Green Beans (page 178) or Mom's Coleslaw (page 181) are cooling accompaniments.

serves 6

¾ cup plus 1 tablespoon olive oil

1 cup all-purpose flour

1 pound smoked sausage, such as Cajun sausage, kielbasa, or hot links, sliced ½ inch thick

3 cups chopped green bell peppers (about 2)

3 cups chopped celery

1 large onion, chopped

3 garlic cloves, minced

Two 14.5-ounce cans diced tomatoes with jalapeños

5½ cups chicken broth

¼ teaspoon cayenne pepper, or to taste

1 teaspoon freshly ground black pepper

1 teaspoon dried thyme

1 teaspoon dried oregano

1. Make the roux: In a saucepan combine the ¾ cup oil and the flour. Cook the mixture over moderately high heat, whisking constantly, until it begins to brown and smells like popcorn. Reduce the heat to medium and continue cooking and whisking until the mixture resembles chocolate sauce. The whole process should take 10 to 12 minutes.

The roux can be made 2 days in advance, covered, and chilled.

2. In a large, heavy-bottomed pot, cook the sausage in the 1 tablespoon oil over moderate heat for 5 minutes. Reserve 1 cup each of the bell pepper and celery, and add the remainder to the pot with the onion and garlic. Cook, stirring, until the vegetables are softened. Stir in the roux, tomatoes with their juice, chicken broth, cayenne, black pepper, thyme, oregano, and bay leaf, and bring the gumbo to a boil, stirring. Add the okra and reserved bell pepper and celery, and simmer for 20 minutes. Remove the bay leaf.

The gumbo can be made up to this point 2 days in advance. Let it cool completely and keep covered and chilled.

1 bay leaf

½ pound okra, sliced

1 pint shucked oysters (about
16), including their liquor,
checked for shell fragments

2 cups cooked rice as an
accompaniment

3. Just before serving, stir in the oysters with their liquid and simmer for 3 minutes. Serve over a spoonful of cooked rice.

Note: The brown roux used here is a standard Cajun ingredient used in many dishes. It adds thickening, color, and a deep nutty flavor. Filé powder is classically used in gumbo as an additional thickener, but it is difficult to find in many places and personally I don't miss it here.

fried oysters on watercress salad
with honey balsamic dressing

Crisp, hot fried oysters, tangy watercress, and creamy goat cheese make this a satisfying salad of tastes and textures. For hints on frying, see the note on page 145. Serve this as a light lunch or supper with a soup perhaps, or as an appetizer.

serves 4 as a main course
or 6 as an appetizer

1 pint shucked oysters (about 16), including their liquor, checked for shell fragments

½ cup milk

2 tablespoons balsamic vinegar

1 teaspoon honey

2 teaspoons Dijon mustard

¼ teaspoon salt

¼ teaspoon black pepper

3 tablespoons extra virgin olive oil

for frying the oysters

4 to 8 cups vegetable oil

½ cup cornmeal

¾ cup all-purpose flour

¾ teaspoon salt

1. Strain the oyster liquor into a small, heavy saucepan. In a bowl soak the oysters in the milk, cover, and refrigerate. Boil the oyster liquor until it is reduced to 2 tablespoons.

2. In a small bowl, whisk together the vinegar, honey, mustard, salt, pepper, and reduced oyster liquor. Add the olive oil in a stream, whisking until it is emulsified.

3. In a heavy pot or deep fryer, heat at least 3 inches of vegetable oil until it registers between 375°F and 380°F on a deep-fat or candy thermometer.

4. While the oil is heating, in a large plastic or paper bag combine the cornmeal, flour, salt, and pepper, and shake to blend. Lift one handful of oysters from the bowl, letting the excess milk drip off, and put them in the bag. Holding the top closed, shake the oysters until they are coated with the flour mixture. Drop the oysters into the oil and fry until pale golden, about 1 minute. With a slotted spoon, transfer to brown paper to drain. Fry the remaining oysters in the same

¼ teaspoon freshly ground
  black pepper
4 cups watercress sprigs,
  rinsed and spun dry
⅓ cup crumbled mild goat
  cheese

manner, working in small batches and allowing the oil to return to 380°F before adding the next batch.

5. In a large bowl, toss the watercress with half the dressing and divide among plates. Top with the oysters and drizzle with the remaining dressing. Sprinkle with the goat cheese.

fried oyster sandwich with parsley, caesar mayonnaise, and tomatoes

The tastiest fried oysters I have ever had were in New Orleans. When they pile those plump crisp morsels between bread, they call it a Po' Boy, and that's where the inspiration for this sandwich came from. For hints on frying, see the note on page 145. To make a complete meal, serve the sandwiches with Mom's Coleslaw (page 181) or Potato Salad with Roasted Peppers and Sesame Seeds (page 169).

makes 2 sandwiches

¼ cup mayonnaise

1 teaspoon dry mustard

1 teaspoon Worcestershire sauce

18 shucked oysters (about 18 ounces), drained and checked for shell fragments

½ cup milk

4 to 8 cups vegetable oil for frying

½ cup cornmeal

¾ cup all-purpose flour

¾ teaspoon salt

¼ teaspoon freshly ground black pepper

A 12-inch soft baguette

½ cup shredded lettuce, such as iceberg or romaine

1 tomato, thinly sliced

1. In a small bowl, stir together the mayonnaise, mustard, and Worcestershire sauce.

2. Pour off any excess liquid from the oysters and add the milk, coating them well.

3. In a large, heavy pot or deep-fryer, heat at least 3 inches of oil until it registers between 375°F and 380°F on a deep-fat or candy thermometer.

4. While the oil is heating, in a large plastic or paper bag combine the cornmeal, flour, salt, and pepper, and shake to blend. Lift one handful of oysters from the bowl, letting the excess milk drip off, and put them in the bag. Holding the top closed, shake the oysters until they are coated with the flour mixture. Drop the oysters into the oil and fry until pale golden, about 1 minute. With a slotted spoon, transfer to brown paper to drain. Fry the remaining oysters in the same manner, working in small batches and allowing the oil to return to 380°F before adding the next batch.

5. Split the baguette lengthwise and spread it with the mayonnaise mixture. Arrange the oysters on one cut side and top with the lettuce and tomato. Close the bread and cut the sandwich in half. Serve immediately.

sautéed oysters with cider butter sauce

Sweet, sour, nutty, and rich, these oysters are perfect cold-weather fare. Serve with plain noodles or Two Potato Hash (page 170), Roasted Maple Butter Acorn Squash (page 177), and Quick Pickled Green Beans (page 178).

serves 2 as a main course
and 4 as an appetizer

24 shucked oysters (about 24 ounces), including their liquor, checked for shell fragments

1¼ cups apple cider

2 tablespoons red or white wine vinegar

1 large shallot, finely chopped

7 tablespoons butter

1 tablespoon olive oil

All-purpose flour for dredging the oysters

¼ cup coarsely chopped walnuts, lightly toasted

¼ cup chopped fresh parsley

1. Drain the oysters, catching the liquor in a saucepan, and reserve the oysters, chilled. Add the cider, vinegar, and shallot to the saucepan, and boil the liquid until it is reduced to ⅓ cup. Remove the pan from the heat and whisk in 6 tablespoons of the butter, 1 tablespoon at a time, returning the pan to the heat only long enough to rewarm the sauce. Whisk in salt and pepper to taste, and keep warm.

2. In a large nonstick skillet, heat the remaining 1 tablespoon butter and the oil over moderately high heat until the foam subsides. Working in batches, coat each oyster with flour and add it to the skillet. Sauté for 1 minute on each side, or until the edges curl.

3. Divide the oysters among plates, top with the cider sauce, and sprinkle with the walnuts and parsley.

oysters in lemon sauce

These oysters, which are simmered briefly in a smooth, creamy lemon sauce, are delicious alone or spooned over cooked fettuccine or egg noodles. On the side, serve Sliced Asparagus and Edamame with Olive Oil (page 176), and Green Salad with Creamy Mustard Dressing and Sweet and Spicy Pecans (page 184), or Spinach Salad with Blue Cheese and Plum Dressing (page 186).

serves 4

¾ cup chopped shallots
(about 3 medium shallots)

3 tablespoons butter

3 tablespoons all-purpose
flour

1 cup milk

2 large egg yolks

½ teaspoon freshly grated
lemon zest

¼ cup fresh lemon juice

1 teaspoon Tabasco or other
hot sauce

1 pint shucked oysters (about
16), drained well and
checked for shell fragments

2 tablespoons minced fresh
parsley

1. In a medium saucepan, cook the shallots in the butter over moderate heat until soft, about 5 minutes. Stir in the flour and cook, stirring, for 2 minutes. Add the milk and bring to a boil, whisking.

2. In a small bowl, whisk together the egg yolks, lemon zest and juice, and Tabasco. Whisk into the sauce and bring to a simmer, whisking constantly for 2 minutes (the sauce will be very thick, like pudding). Add the oysters to the saucepan and cook, stirring gently over moderate heat, until the edges of the oysters curl and the sauce begins to simmer. Stir in the parsley and salt and pepper to taste.

3. Serve immediately as is, or over pasta, with additional Tabasco on the side.

oyster stew

Every Christmas Eve, as long as I can remember, my mother has reached for her stained, yellowed, well-used copy of Craig Claiborne's New York Times Cookbook *(1961) and opened it to page 76—Oyster Stew. Picking up the freshly shucked oysters from the fish market was the most important chore of the day. My crucial job in the kitchen was to make sure the double boiler, which heated the pan of cream, butter, and oysters, never got above a gentle simmer. Over the years I have made some minor changes, like using half-and-half instead of the original milk-cream combination, and seasoning with hot Hungarian paprika, but that has not changed the fact that one spoonful of this soup still brings me back to my childhood Christmas.*

makes about 4 cups; serves 4

½ stick (4 tablespoons) butter

1 pint shucked oysters (about 16), including their liquor, checked for shell fragments

2 cups half-and-half

½ teaspoon salt

¼ teaspoon hot Hungarian paprika or black pepper to taste

2 tablespoons minced fresh parsley

In a double boiler or a metal bowl set over a pan of simmering water, heat the butter, oysters with their liquor, half-and-half, salt, and paprika until hot and the oysters float to the top. Do not let the stew boil or it will curdle. Serve immediately.

Note: Simple oyster stews originally were cooked by the people who harvested the oysters. The stews offered warmth and nourishment with the few ingredients available to them. Oyster crackers were eventually served alongside, to be crumbled into the soup for thickening and bulk.

oyster and corn soup

This smooth corn soup gets its richness from corn rather than cream, making it taste more decadent than it actually is. And the smoky hot roasted jalapeños balance the sweetness of the corn. As roasting intensifies their "heat," add the chiles to the soup gradually, tasting as you go, to achieve the desired spiciness or pass them separately, to be added by the diner as desired.

makes about 7 cups;
serves 6 to 8 as a first course
or 4 as a light supper

4 ears fresh corn, shucked

1 teaspoon ground cumin or
   whole cumin seeds

1 bay leaf

3 large jalapeño chiles

1 pint shucked oysters (about
   16), including their liquor,
   checked for shell fragments

2 cups milk

1. With a sharp knife, cut the kernels from the corn and add them with the cobs to a large saucepan with 3 cups water, the cumin, and bay leaf. Simmer, covered, for 30 minutes.

2. Meanwhile, roast the jalapeños by holding them with tongs over an open flame, or set them on a cooling rack on an electric burner. Turn them as the skins blister and char until they are completely blackened. Wrap them in a paper towel for 5 minutes; then, using the towel, rub off the skins. Split the jalapeños in half, removing the seeds and stems, and finely chop them.

3. Remove the corncobs and let them cool until they can be handled. With the back edge of a knife, scrape the cobs into the pot, and discard the cobs.

4. Discard the bay leaf and in a blender puree the corn soup until smooth. Pour the puree through a fine sieve set over a saucepan, pressing hard on the solids.

The soup can be made up to this point a day in advance, covered, and refrigerated.

5. Add the oysters with their liquor and the milk, and heat the soup until it is hot and the oysters float, but do not let it boil. Stir in the jalapeños and salt to taste, and serve the soup immediately.

Note: Frozen corn is not a suitable substitute, as it contains less of the starch and therefore less of the thickening power of fresh corn.

oyster soup with coconut milk, chiles, lime, and cilantro

Southeast Asian cooking uses coconut milk to enrich sauces, soups, and stews in the same way that French cuisine uses cream. Hot chile and sour citrus contrast with the smooth, slightly sweet nutty flavor of both the milk and the oysters. Serve with plain steamed rice, Grapefruit Rice with Chives (page 171), Sliced Asparagus and Edamame with Olive Oil (page 176), or Potato Salad with Roasted Peppers and Sesame Seeds (page 169).

makes about 3½ cups; serves 2 to 4

1 pint shucked oysters (about 16), including their liquor, checked for shell fragments

1 cup bottled clam juice or shell stock (see page 4)

1½ cups canned unsweetened coconut milk (see Note)

1 jalapeño chile, quartered lengthwise

3 scallions (a.k.a. green onions), thinly sliced

Zest of ½ lime, removed with a vegetable peeler and minced

2 tablespoons fresh lime juice

¼ cup packed chopped fresh basil

¼ cup packed chopped fresh cilantro

1 teaspoon salt, or to taste

1. Strain the oysters over a saucepan, and reserve the oysters. To the oyster liquor add the clam juice, coconut milk, jalapeño, scallions, and lime zest, and simmer 5 minutes.

2. Add the oysters and lime juice, and simmer gently until the oyster edges curl, about 2 minutes. Stir in the basil, cilantro, and salt, and serve immediately.

Note: *As the cuisines of Southeast Asia have become more popular, ingredients have become more readily available. Canned coconut milk can be found on many supermarket shelves, cutting out the labor-intensive process of soaking grated coconut with hot water, then squeezing the coconut dry. Make sure you use unsweetened coconut milk, not to be confused with the syrupy cream of coconut used to make piña coladas.*

lobster

maine

In the early seventeenth century, lobsters were so plentiful on the East Coast of the United States, they were considered food for the poor. Pots and lobstermen were not necessary, as the crustaceans were gathered by hand along the shore. In the mid–1800s, increased demand, and the practice of canning lobster meat for shipping long distances, depleted the lobster population and what was once an everyday food became a delicacy.

The **Maine** or American lobster is found in the cold mid- to north Atlantic waters. It has a smooth green, brown, and black shell (which turns bright orange after cooking), and two powerful front claws, usually secured with thick rubber bands in markets. A live lobster should be picked up by grasping it by its back shell, where it is impossible for the claws to reach. The meat is rich, briny, and slightly sweet, with a pleasant silky yet chewy texture. The green tomalley (liver) and red roe (in the female) are edible.

purchasing

Maine lobsters are best when purchased live, but many stores offer fresh cooked, picked meat. Recently available, and quite good, are frozen raw tails, frozen whole cooked lobsters, or cooked and vacuum-packed lobster meat. A new high-pressure process has been used to retrieve raw meat easily from the shell, and is used in restaurants and food service. Some frozen canned lobster meat can be of good quality, while others have a spongy texture when thawed.

The minimum legal size for a lobster is determined by the length of its back shell, but in the market it is categorized by weight. Usually they are sorted and priced by weight; 1¼- to 1½-pounders, 1½- to 2-pounders, 2- to 3-pounders, and so on. "Chicken" lobsters are the smallest (between 1 pound and 1¼ pounds), and "culls" have one claw or one small claw.

Generally you pay more per pound for lobsters weighing more than 1¼ pounds. I have heard many reasons for this, such as there is more meat per pound in heavier lobsters or the meat in large lobsters is sweeter than that of small ones, none of which are true. The reason for the price difference is because there are many more small lobsters than large ones. It's simply the result of supply and demand. Live lobsters can survive out of water in a bag, kept refrigerated, for several days.

spiny

The warm-water **spiny**, **rock**, **Florida**, or **Caribbean** lobster has a thick and spiky shell, and there are no large front claws. These lobsters are eaten for their tail meat only. The meat is very similar to that of Maine lobster, though slightly less sweet. The texture is rougher and slightly more tender, and it is less chewy than Maine lobster.

purchasing

Spiny lobster is most commonly sold as frozen tails, unless you live where they are harvested. In the past, "lobster tails" for sale meant tails from the spiny lobster, but recently, frozen Maine lobster tails have appeared on the market. Fresh spiny lobster is available most often in California and Florida, from early fall through early spring.

approximate yields for lobster

Keep in mind that the amount of meat inside a lobster can vary. In the summer months, when lobsters are molting, the meat can be much smaller than the shell, or if a lobster is stressed or has been without food, you can have a smaller yield. There is no way to determine this before cooking.

1¼- TO 1½-POUND COOKED MAINE LOBSTER EQUALS

- 5 to 7 ounces (170g) meat
- 1 cup diced meat
- 3 frozen lobster tails (4 ounces each)

5-POUND MAINE LOBSTER EQUALS

- 1 pound meat

raw lobster meat

The easiest way to obtain raw lobster meat is by removing it from thawed, frozen lobster tails. This can also be done by cutting a live lobster in half, but this takes some guts, practice, and confidence, and is not a technique used in this book.

to boil lobster

Make sure you have a large enough pot to hold the lobster(s) and bring about 4 inches of water to a rapid boil. Add the lobsters, cover, and return to the boil. Start timing according to the chart, and reduce the heat slightly to keep it from boiling over.

1-pounders—8 minutes

1¼-pounders—9 minutes

2-pounders—12 minutes

6-pounders—17 minutes

do lobsters feel pain?

There are many techniques that have been developed to make people feel better about cooking live lobster. Whether you start a lobster in boiling water or warm water or hypnotize it before cooking, a lobster has no brain or complex central nervous system and therefore cannot process pain.

northeast lobster salad for "lobster rolls"

As a child, I began eating lobster rolls at a place called Lunch. I always thought it had no name, and the big LUNCH sign was an advertisement for what it served. We would take a break from the beach in Amagansett, Long Island, and head to this rustic diner at the edge of busy Montauk Highway. Toasted soft, white hot dog rolls were mounded with generous, luscious chunks of lobster meat, bound with mayonnaise and some other barely noticeable ingredients, and served with unremarkable potato chips. I realize now what a treat it was, but at the time I thought I was eating what every other hot, sandy, salty kid eats in the summertime.

serves 2 to 3

About 1¼ cups (8 to
  10 ounces) chopped
  cooked lobster meat
  (see page 123)
¼ cup mayonnaise
⅓ cup chopped celery
2 tablespoons chopped
  scallions (a.k.a. green
  onions)
1 teaspoon Dijon mustard
2 or 3 hot dog buns
  (preferably the kind with flat
  sides), lightly toasted and
  buttered

In a medium bowl, gently stir together the lobster, mayonnaise, celery, scallions, mustard, and salt and pepper to taste. Fill the buns with the salad and serve.

Note: This salad can be fancied up by serving it in an avocado half or a hollowed-out tomato.

lobster sushi salad

This warm-weather salad includes the flavors of a California roll, but uses lobster in place of surimi or crab. Short- or medium-grain rice produces a stickier rice than long grain, and when it is tossed with mild rice vinegar, the grains get shiny and maintain a chewy texture. Experiment with different fresh vegetables, such as corn, tomatoes, or squash, to find your own favorite combination. Sliced Asparagus and Edamame with Olive Oil (page 176) and Sprouts and Sliced Tomato Salad (page 179) are delicious on the side.

serves 4

1 cup "sushi" rice (medium- or short-grain white rice)

½ cup seasoned rice vinegar

½ to 1 teaspoon prepared wasabi (green Japanese horseradish; see Note)

¼ cup vegetable oil

¾ to 1 pound (about 2 cups) diced cooked lobster meat (see page 123)

1 ripe avocado

1 large cucumber, halved, seeded, and cut lengthwise into thin strips

1 tablespoon sesame seeds

1. In a small, heavy saucepan, combine the rice and 1¼ cups water, and bring to a boil. Stir once, cover, and reduce the heat to a rapid simmer. Simmer for 15 minutes, or until the water is absorbed. Remove from the heat and let rest for 5 minutes. Transfer the rice to a bowl, fluffing it, add ¼ cup of the vinegar and toss with a rubber spatula until almost cool. (The grains of rice will become shiny and separate as you toss.)

2. In a small bowl, whisk together the remaining ¼ cup vinegar and wasabi to taste. Add the oil and whisk until emulsified.

3. Divide the rice among four plates, making a well in the center. Toss the lobster with 2 tablespoons of the dressing and spoon on top of the rice. Peel, pit, and slice the avocado, and arrange it and the cucumber strips around the lobster, and drizzle with the remaining dressing. Sprinkle with the sesame seeds.

The salads can be prepared up to 30 minutes in advance, covered, and refrigerated.

Note: Wasabi, the green pungent paste most familiar to people as an accompaniment to sushi, is widely available in the international sections of many supermarkets. Wasabi can be bought as powder in a jar, and must be mixed with water to form a paste (follow the directions on the packaging). Wasabi is also sold already prepared in a paste.

lobster, mango, and jicama salad
with jalapeño yogurt dressing

This dish offers a tropical twist on the traditional mayonnaise-based salad. Sweet mango, crisp ji-cama, yogurt, and chiles add a bright and tangy flavor to rich, briny lobster. One bite of this salad, with its bright tropical flavors, can conjure up palm trees and warm breezes. Serve on a bed of lettuce with Summer Corn on the Cob with Basil Butter (page 175) and Grapefruit Rice with Chives (page 171).

serves 4

¼ cup plain yogurt

¼ cup mayonnaise

2 tablespoons fresh lime juice

1 large jalapeño or serrano chile, seeded and chopped, reserving some of the seeds (see Note)

1 pound (about 2 cups) diced cooked lobster meat (see page 123)

½ small jicama, peeled and diced (about 1 cup)

1 large ripe mango, peeled and diced

¼ cup finely chopped red onions

1 tablespoon minced fresh cilantro (optional)

1. In a salad bowl, whisk together the yogurt, mayonnaise, and lime juice. Add the jalapeño to taste, adding the chopped seeds as desired to adjust the spiciness.

2. Add the lobster, jicama, mango, onion, cilantro, if using, and salt to taste, and toss well.

The salad keeps, covered and refrigerated, for up to 36 hours.

Note: Most of the heat in chiles is in the seeds, but it varies greatly from chile to chile. Reserve the seeds so you can add the desired amount of spice.

asian lobster and noodle salad

The lively flavors of ginger, rice vinegar, and cayenne are softened with creamy peanut butter in this Chinese-inspired salad. Protein, vegetable, and starch are all there. Just serve and enjoy.

serves 2 as a main course
or 4 as an appetizer

2 tablespoons peanut butter

¼ cup seasoned rice vinegar

1 teaspoon soy sauce

⅓ cup vegetable oil

½ teaspoon sugar

1 tablespoon minced peeled
   fresh ginger

⅛ to ¼ teaspoon cayenne
   pepper

¼ pound vermicelli or angel
   hair pasta

¼ pound snow peas, cut into
   ½-inch slices

1¼ cups (8 to 10 ounces)
   chopped cooked lobster
   meat, including any red roe
   (see page 123)

½ medium cucumber, peeled
   and cut into thin julienne
   strips

⅓ cup chopped scallions
   (a.k.a. green onions)

¼ cup chopped fresh cilantro

1. In a large bowl, whisk until smooth the peanut butter, rice vinegar, and soy sauce. Add the oil, sugar, ginger, and cayenne to taste and whisk until smooth.

2. In a pot of boiling salted water, cook the vermicelli for 1 minute less than the manufacturer's directions. Add the snow peas and boil 1 minute, or until the pasta is tender. Rinse under cold water and drain well. Transfer to the bowl and toss with the dressing.

3. Add the lobster with any minced roe, the cucumber, scallions, cilantro, and salt to taste, and toss well.

bllts (bacon, lobster, lettuce, and tomato sandwiches)

Need to impress? Make a friend? Influence someone? Serve these sandwiches. They are close-your-eyes-and-moan yummy! Alongside, try Red, White, and Blue Slaw (page 183) or Quick Pickled Green Beans (page 178).

**makes 2 large
or 4 small sandwiches**

¼ cup mayonnaise

1 tablespoon fresh lemon
   juice

¼ teaspoon freshly ground
   black pepper

2 large croissants or 4 small
   croissants

About 1¼ cups (8 to
   10 ounces) chopped
   cooked lobster meat
   (see page 123)

4 slices tomato

4 large pieces romaine or
   Bibb lettuce, washed and
   spun dry

4 slices crisp cooked bacon

1. In a small bowl, stir together the mayonnaise, lemon juice, and pepper.

2. Halve the croissants and spread the cut sides with the mayonnaise mixture. Divide the lobster, tomato, lettuce, and bacon among the croissants, press the sandwiches closed, and cut them in half.

lobster, asparagus, and goat cheese strata

Here is a special-occasion breakfast, brunch, or lunch dish, perfect for a party or overnight guests. Savory bread puddings (a.k.a. stratas) need time to rest in the refrigerator, in order for the bread to soak up the egg and milk. After a night of soaking it is ready to pop in the oven, but beware, when you pull this golden puffed masterpiece from the oven, your guests may never go home! Green Salad with Grapes and Sunflower Seeds (page 187) makes a nice accompaniment, no matter what time of day.

serves 6 to 8

1 large onion, sliced (about
2 cups)

2 tablespoons butter

¾ pound asparagus, rinsed,
trimmed, and cut into
1-inch lengths

2 celery ribs, sliced (about
2 cups)

2 regular-size plain English
muffins, split in half

¾ pound coarsely chopped
cooked lobster (see
page 123) or crabmeat,
rinsed and picked over for
bits of cartilage and shell
(about 2 cups)

4 ounces crumbled goat
cheese (about ¾ cup)

6 large eggs

1½ cups milk

½ teaspoon salt

½ teaspoon freshly ground
black pepper

1. Butter a 9-inch square baking pan or dish.

2. In a large skillet, cook the onion in the butter over moderate heat until softened, about 10 minutes. Add the asparagus and celery and cook, stirring, for 2 minutes. (The asparagus should still be crisp.) Let cool.

3. Arrange the English muffin halves in the baking pan, cut sides up. Scatter the lobster meat on the muffins, and top with the vegetable mixture and goat cheese. Whisk together the eggs, milk, salt, and pepper, and pour over the ingredients in the pan.

4. Refrigerate the pudding, covered, for 8 to 24 hours.

5. Preheat the oven to 375°F.

6. Bake the pudding, uncovered, for 45 minutes, or until set in the middle, puffed, and golden. Cut into squares and serve immediately.

whole lobsters

I must admit I am a purist when it comes to lobster. Freshly steamed with a bowl of melted butter is how I was raised to eat them. But sometimes I crave something different, especially if I'm entertaining. The following two recipes offer slight twists on the classic, but the way you get to the lobster meat is still the same.

how to serve a whole lobster

Give diners a head start with their lobster and reduce some of the messiness at the table by detaching the tail from the body and splitting open the bodies with a sharp knife between the small feeler claws. Then pull the large claws from the jointed legs and drain any liquid from them by moving the claws open and shut. Pile all the parts of each lobster onto a large plate and serve with a bowl of dipping sauce.

steamed lobsters with orange butter

This orange sauce, flavored with garlic and spiked with red pepper flakes, offers a special twist without straying too far from the classic. The sauce is also delicious as a dip for artichokes. I can't imagine having lobster without Mom's Coleslaw (page 181) and Summer Corn on the Cob with Basil Butter (page 175).

serves 4

Four 1¼- to 1½-pound live
    lobsters

2 large garlic cloves, minced

1 cup (2 sticks) butter

1 cup dry white wine

Grated zest of 1 orange

¼ teaspoon hot red pepper
    flakes

1 cup fresh orange juice

1 teaspoon all-purpose flour

1. In a pot large enough to hold the lobsters, cook the garlic in 2 tablespoons of the butter over moderate heat until it begins to turn golden. Add the wine and 2 cups water, and bring to a boil. Add the lobsters head first, return to the boil, cover tightly, and cook for 10 minutes. (Reduce the heat slightly, if necessary, to keep the pot from boiling over.)

2. Transfer the lobsters with tongs to a platter, and keep warm, covered with aluminum foil.

3. Transfer the cooking liquid to a small saucepan, add the orange zest and pepper flakes, and boil until reduced to ½ cup. Add the orange juice and boil until reduced to about ¾ cup. Whisk together the flour and 1 tablespoon water, and add to the sauce, whisking for 2 minutes. Add the remaining butter a little at a time, whisking, until the sauce is smooth. Season with salt to taste.

4. Serve the lobsters with the sauce in individual dipping bowls (see page 132 for how to serve a whole lobster).

lobsters with vodka and tarragon butter sauce

My neighbor gave me this recipe and I thank him for the many times he's been there with a cup of sugar, or vodka, when I'm out. This is a slightly more sophisticated way to enjoy steamed lobster, but down-home side dishes still apply: Carolina Vinegar Slaw (page 182) or Red, White, and Blue Slaw (page 183), and Two Potato Hash (page 170).

serves 2

1 cup vodka

Two 1¼- to 1½-pound live
    Maine lobsters

1 tablespoon chopped fresh
    tarragon

¼ cup minced shallots

6 tablespoons butter

1. In a pot large enough to hold the lobsters, bring the vodka and 2 cups water to a boil. Add the lobsters head first, return to the boil, cover tightly, and cook for 10 minutes. (Reduce the heat slightly, if necessary, to keep the pot from boiling over.)

2. Transfer the lobsters with tongs to a platter, and keep warm, covered with aluminum foil.

3. Transfer the cooking liquid to a small saucepan and add the tarragon and shallot. Boil until the liquid is reduced to about 3 tablespoons.

4. Remove the saucepan from the heat and whisk in the butter, a little at a time, to form a smooth sauce. (Return the pan to the heat for a moment if the sauce is not hot enough to melt the butter, but do not boil or the sauce will separate.) Season with salt and pepper to taste and serve immediately, in individual dipping bowls, with the lobsters (see page 132 for how to serve a whole lobster).

caribbean-style grilled lobster

Grilling lobster is tricky, because it can dry out quickly. I am most familiar with boiled lobster from the cold Northeast, but in the beautiful tropical setting of the Caribbean, a split whole rock lobster is irresistible when grilled over hot coals and basted with butter. To keep the meat as moist as possible, the shell is split but not halved, and cooking is finished with the cut side up, to retain the juices and butter. For side dishes serve fresh steamed vegetables, Mom's Coleslaw (page 181), Potato Salad with Roasted Peppers and Sesame Seeds (page 169), Baked Vegetable and Cheese Polenta (page 174), or Summer Corn on the Cob with Basil Butter (page 175).

serves 4

4 large rock lobster tails
(6 to 7 ounces each) or
8 small (3 to 4 ounces
each), defrosted if frozen
½ stick (4 tablespoons) butter
1 tablespoon fresh lemon
juice
½ teaspoon Tabasco or other
hot sauce

1. With a sharp knife, cut through the underside of each lobster tail, splitting it but not cutting through the back shell. Holding each tail in a kitchen towel, spread the two halves apart until the back shell just cracks, exposing the meat slightly.

2. In a small saucepan, melt the butter with the lemon juice and Tabasco.

3. To grill: On a preheated grill, cook the tails, slit side down, for 3 minutes for small tails and 5 minutes for large. Turn the tails, spoon some of the butter on top, and grill 3 to 5 minutes more, basting with more butter until just cooked through (see Note).

To broil: Arrange the tails in a shallow baking pan, slit sides down, and broil about 4 inches from the heat for 3 minutes for small tails and 5 minutes for large. Turn the tails, spoon some of the butter on top, and broil 3 to 5 minutes more, brushing with more butter until cooked just through (see Note).

4. Serve immediately.

Note: It is very important not to overcook the lobster. When it is almost cooked through, but still looks slightly raw in the center, remove it from the heat. The heat from the shell and surrounding meat will cook it through. You can always put it on the heat for another 30 seconds if it still seems underdone.

spicy tomato and lobster linguine

If you serve this to guests do not tell them how easy it is—you want them to be impressed! Just smile. Crusty bread and Eggless Caesar Salad (page 188) are a must.

serves 4

3 garlic cloves, minced

⅓ cup olive oil

Two 14.5-ounce cans diced
   tomatoes with jalapeños

1 cup whole, pitted black
   California olives

Two 1¼-pound live Maine
   lobsters

½ pound linguine or
   spaghetti

2 tablespoons chopped fresh
   tarragon, basil, or parsley

1. In a pot large enough to hold the lobsters, cook the garlic in the oil over moderate heat until it begins to turn golden. Add the tomatoes and olives, and bring to a boil. Add the lobsters, cover tightly, and cook them at a gentle boil for 15 minutes. Transfer the lobsters to a cutting board.

2. In a pot of boiling salted water, boil the linguine until just tender and drain well. Add the pasta to the tomato sauce and toss well.

3. Split the lobster tails, remove and slice the meat. Divide the pasta among plates and top with the lobster meat. Crack the lobster claws and knuckles, and divide them among the plates. Sprinkle each dish with some of the tarragon. Serve immediately.

lobster, asparagus, and yellow pepper risotto

Risotto is made with a starchy, short-grain rice that absorbs liquid until it is plump and creamy. It is worth investing the time to make a lobster stock from the steaming liquid and shells, because it adds additional intense lobster flavor. This is also a great way to stretch a little lobster to serve many. Green Salad with Grapes and Sunflower Seeds (page 187) or Eggless Caesar Salad (page 188) is all that's needed to complete the meal.

serves 4 to 6

½ cup sliced shallots

2 tablespoons butter

1 cup Arborio, Risotto, or
   Carnaroli rice

½ cup dry white wine

5 cups hot lobster shell stock
   (page 4) or bottled clam
   juice

⅓ pound asparagus, washed
   and cut into 1-inch pieces
   (about 2 cups)

1 yellow bell pepper, seeded
   and diced

2 to 2½ cups cubed cooked
   lobster meat, including any
   roe (see page 123)

1 tablespoon Cognac or
   2 teaspoons lemon juice

¼ cup freshly grated
   Parmesan

3 tablespoons chopped fresh
   basil leaves

1. In a large, heavy saucepan, cook the shallots in the butter over moderate heat, stirring, until softened, about 10 minutes. Add the rice and cook, stirring, for 1 minute. Add the wine and boil until almost evaporated.

2. Keep the lobster stock hot in another saucepan. Add ½ cup of it to the rice and boil it, stirring often, until it is nearly absorbed, about 2 minutes. Keep adding the stock by ½ cups and boiling until absorbed until there is about 1 cup of stock remaining. Stir in the asparagus, bell pepper, and any minced lobster roe, and continue adding the stock in the same way until it is all used.

The rice should be tender but not mushy, and the mixture should be like a thick soup. Total cooking time will be 20 to 23 minutes.

3. Stir in the lobster, Cognac, Parmesan, basil, and salt and pepper to taste. Serve immediately.

Note: Risotto is a delicious treat for company, but it needs to be served immediately. All of the ingredients can be prepared ahead of time, but the cooking needs to be done all at once.

lobster chardonnay with mushrooms and peas

*T*his is a great way to serve lobster to guests without breaking the bank. If you really want to impress, make individual pies in large ramekins and cover them with rounds of puff pastry. Serve with Green Salad with Creamy Mustard Dressing and Sweet and Spicy Pecans (page 184), Green Salad with Grapes and Sunflower Seeds (page 187), or Eggless Caesar Salad (page 188).

serves 4 to 6

1 cup chopped onions

3 tablespoons butter

⅓ cup all-purpose flour

1 cup Chardonnay or other
   dry white wine

2 cups lobster shell stock (see
   page 4), lobster cooking
   water, or bottled clam juice

8 ounces white mushrooms,
   wiped clean and sliced

¾ cup chopped celery (about
   2 ribs)

1 teaspoon dried thyme or
   1 tablespoon fresh

½ teaspoon dried tarragon or
   2 teaspoons fresh

1 pound medium egg noodles

1 cup frozen peas

¾ cup heavy cream

2½ cups cubed cooked
   lobster meat, including any
   roe (see page 123)

¼ cup chopped fresh parsley

1. In a deep, heavy skillet, cook the onion in the butter over moderate heat, stirring, until softened, about 5 minutes. Add the flour and cook, stirring, for 1 minute. Whisk in the wine and lobster stock, and bring to a boil, whisking. Stir in the mushrooms, celery, thyme, and tarragon, and simmer for 8 minutes, stirring occasionally.

The mixture can be made up to this point up in advance. If holding for more than 30 minutes, cool and refrigerate, covered, for up to 4 hours.

2. In a pot of boiling salted water, cook the noodles until just tender and drain.

3. Stir the peas and cream into the sauce and bring to a boil. Stir in the lobster and salt and pepper to taste, and serve over the noodles, sprinkled with the parsley.

Note: Shrimp, crab, crayfish, and scallops all make perfect substitutes for the lobster.

citrus lobster bisque with chives

I *love the combination of citrus and shellfish. The sweet-and-sour nature of zesty fruits deliciously complements briny rich fruits of the sea. This bisque is an extra treat the day after (or days after) a lobster dinner. Save the lobster shells and cooking liquid for the making a simple stock and use it for the base of this luxurious soup.*

makes about 6 cups; serves 4 to 6

1 leek, washed well (see Note) and finely chopped

½ stick (4 tablespoons) butter

Grated zest of 1 orange (about 1 tablespoon)

Grated zest of ½ lemon (about ½ teaspoon)

⅔ cup all-purpose flour

4 cups lobster shell stock (see page 4) or bottled clam juice

¾ cup fresh-squeezed orange juice

1 tablespoon sweet paprika

1⅓ cups half-and-half

Chopped cooked lobster meat, if desired (see page 123)

2 tablespoons minced fresh chives

1. In a large, heavy saucepan, cook the leek in the butter with the orange and lemon zests over moderately low heat, stirring occasionally, until softened, about 15 minutes.

2. Stir in the flour and cook, stirring, for 2 minutes. Add the stock, orange juice, and paprika, and simmer, stirring, for 5 minutes. Stir in the half-and-half, lobster meat, if using, and salt and pepper to taste, and heat until hot. Serve sprinkled with the chives.

The bisque can be frozen in an airtight container for up to 4 months.

Notes: To clean leeks, trim the root ends and tough green leaves from the leeks. Split each lengthwise, leaving them attached at the root end, and rub the grit out of each layer, holding the leek upside down under running water.

Bisques are technically a smooth essence of shellfish soup, but if I have leftover lobster meat, I add it.

lobster and snow pea soup

The extra green taste in this soup comes from the snow pea pods. The fresh and light-tasting puree is a delicious contrast to the rich, sweet, briny lobster pieces. Serve this as a first course or a light supper with bread and Green Salad with Creamy Mustard Dressing and Sweet and Spicy Pecans (page 184) or Green Salad with Grapes and Sunflower Seeds (page 187).

makes about 5 cups; serves 2 to 4

1 medium onion, chopped
(about 1½ cups)

3 tablespoons butter

1 cup diced peeled boiling
potatoes (about 2 small)

3 cups lobster cooking broth,
shell stock (see page 4), or
bottled clam juice

1 pound fresh snow peas,
rinsed

1 tablespoon chopped fresh
mint or 1 teaspoon dried
mint

1 tablespoon chopped fresh
tarragon or 1 teaspoon
dried tarragon

1 cup chopped cooked
lobster meat (see page 123)

Sour cream as an
accompaniment

1. In a large, heavy saucepan, cook the onion in the butter over moderate heat, stirring, for 5 minutes. Add the potatoes and 2½ cups of the broth and simmer, covered, for 6 minutes. Add the snow peas and mint and tarragon, if using dried, and simmer, covered, stirring occasionally, for 8 to 10 minutes, or until the peas are very tender but still bright green. Let the soup cool slightly.

2. In a blender, puree the soup in batches. Strain the puree through a fine sieve set over a bowl, pressing on the solids, and return to the saucepan. Stir in the lobster and mint and tarragon, if using fresh. Heat the soup, thinning with the remaining broth, if desired. Serve with a dollop of sour cream.

Note: Sugar snap peas can be substituted for the snow peas.

squid

a.k.a. calamari

Squid is probably the most underappreciated gift from the sea.
It is a bargain, available year-round, plentiful, and tastes great.
It is sturdy, versatile, and freezes (even refreezes) beautifully. My
personal theory is if we changed its name forever, from squid to
calamari, people would consume it more, with regularity and
enthusiasm.

purchasing

Another major plus for squid is that it is available already cleaned.
The hardest part has already been done when you buy cleaned
frozen sacs and tentacles, or just rings (sliced sacs). Cleaned squid is
also available thawed in many fish markets. Squid is sometimes
available fresh and uncleaned, for those who want the ink for
sauces or pasta, so if you are not sure whether it is cleaned,
just ask.

After thawing squid, feel around inside each sac for any remnant
of a transparent plasticlike quill. This is the animal's shell
(qualifying it for the shellfish category), which sometimes gets left
behind during the cleaning process.

cooking

When considering cooking times for squid, think of it as a lean meat rather than a delicate shellfish. Squid should be cooked very quickly, no more than 2 minutes, to keep it tender (like a thin veal cutlet). Cook it any longer and it will be rubbery. It also tenderizes with long cooking (like a pot roast). Braising squid for at least 20 minutes results in a firm but tender meat.

fried squid with two sauces

This is by far the most popular way to consume squid. In fact, many people believe that "calamari" means fried squid, because it appears on so many menus. Make sure to read the note about oil temperature and enjoy these tender, crispy treats with Red, White, and Blue Slaw (page 183), Carolina Vinegar Slaw (page 182), or Sprouts and Sliced Tomato Salad (page 179).

serves 4 to 6

2½ pounds cleaned squid
    sacs and tentacles,
    defrosted if frozen

½ cup sour cream

½ cup milk

4 to 8 cups vegetable oil for
    deep-frying

2 cups all-purpose flour

2 teaspoons salt

1 teaspoon cayenne pepper

Lemon wedges as an
    accompaniment

Caesar Sour Cream Dip or
    Roasted Pepper and Caper
    Dip (recipes follow)

1. Cut the squid sacs into ½-inch-wide rings and halve the tentacles if they are very large. In a large bowl whisk together the sour cream and milk and add the squid, coating it well.

2. In a heavy pot or deep-fryer, heat at least 3 inches of oil until it registers 380°F on a deep-fat or candy thermometer.

3. In a large bowl, whisk together the flour, salt, and cayenne. Lift about 1 cup, or one handful, of squid from the bowl, letting any excess milk drip off. Add it to the flour and toss to coat the squid. Remove the squid, shaking off the excess flour, fry in the oil until pale golden, about 1 minute, and transfer to brown paper to drain. Fry the remaining squid in the same manner, working in small batches and allowing the oil to return to 380°F before adding the next batch. Keep the squid in a warm oven until all is fried.

4. Serve as soon as possible with lemon wedges and/or one of the sauces.

Note: The key to achieving perfect, tender, fried calamari is the oil. Any vegetable oil will do, but the temperature is crucial. If there is not enough oil, and if it is not at 375°F to 380°F, it will not crisp the squid fast enough. If it does not crisp quickly, the squid loses moisture, shrinks, and becomes tough.

I have been disappointed with many recipes calling for 350°F oil. It just doesn't work on a home stove. Commercial kitchens, with large calibrated fryers that hold gallons of oil at a constant temperature, can fry batch after batch of calamari at 350°F because the temperature doesn't drop dramatically. Electric deep-fryers for home use do a better job at holding the oil temperature, and they contain the mess.

caesar sour cream dip

makes about ⅓ cup

¼ cup sour cream

1½ tablespoons Dijon
   mustard

1 teaspoon Worcestershire
   sauce

½ teaspoon anchovy paste

In a small bowl, stir all of the ingredients together. Keep chilled until ready to use.

roasted pepper and caper dip

makes about ¾ cup

One 7-ounce jar roasted red
   peppers, drained

2 tablespoons drained bottled
   capers

1 small garlic clove

2 tablespoons olive oil

¼ teaspoon salt

Combine all of the ingredients in a blender. Pulse the motor until it forms a coarse puree.

squid and white bean salad

A *simple salad of white beans with herbs and olive oil is a classic Tuscan antipasto selection. The addition of warm tender squid turns a side dish into a satisfying meal. Serve with a good crusty bread and Jollof Rice (page 168) or Baked Vegetable and Cheese Polenta (page 174).*

serves 4 as a main course
or 6 as an appetizer

2 cups canned white beans
(19-ounce can), drained
and rinsed well

2 large garlic cloves, minced

1 cup chopped celery (about
3 ribs)

2 teaspoons minced fresh
thyme

1 teaspoon minced fresh
sage

½ cup fresh lemon juice

½ cup extra virgin olive oil

½ teaspoon hot red pepper
flakes (optional)

1 pound cleaned squid sacs
and tentacles, defrosted if
frozen

1. In a large bowl, gently stir together the beans, garlic, celery, thyme, sage, lemon juice, oil, and pepper flakes, if using.

2. Cut the squid sacs into ¼-inch rings and halve the tentacles. In a saucepan of boiling salted water, cook the squid for 1 minute until opaque and tender. (Overcooking as little as 30 seconds will toughen the squid.) Drain immediately and add to the beans. Toss the salad and let stand for 30 minutes at room temperature before serving. The salad can be kept, covered and refrigerated, up to 2 days.

thai-style squid salad

The fresh, light flavors of ginger, lime, and herbs make this fat-free salad sparkle on the tongue. Serve as an appetizer or turn it into a room-temperature main course by tossing it with thin cooked Asian noodles or spaghetti.

serves 4 as a main course
or 6 as an appetizer

½ cup fresh lime juice

1 tablespoon sugar

1 tablespoon minced peeled
   fresh ginger

1½ teaspoons salt

1 red or yellow bell pepper,
   cut into thin strips

½ cup thinly sliced scallions
   (a.k.a. green onions)

1 small hot chile, minced (see
   Note), or ¼ teaspoon hot
   red pepper flakes

¼ cup chopped fresh mint

¼ cup chopped fresh cilantro

¼ cup chopped fresh basil

1 pound cleaned squid sacs
   and tentacles, defrosted if
   frozen

1. In a salad bowl, stir together the lime juice, sugar, ginger, salt, and 3 tablespoons water. Add the bell pepper, scallions, chile, mint, cilantro, and basil.

2. Cut the squid sacs into ¼-inch rings and halve the tentacles. In a saucepan of boiling salted water, cook the squid for 1 minute until opaque and tender. (Overcooking as little as 30 seconds will toughen the squid.) Drain immediately and add to the herb mixture. Toss the salad and let stand for 30 minutes at room temperature before serving. The salad can be kept, chilled and covered, up to 2 days.

Note: A small, thin red Thai chile can be used in this salad, but a serrano or jalapeño is a good substitute. Beware that most of the "heat" in a chile is in the seeds, and varies in intensity from chile to chile. Mince a whole chile, seeds and all, and add a little bit at a time until the salad has reached the desired spiciness.

stewed squid with moroccan flavors, chickpeas, and raisins

The interesting mix of spices used in this dish is borrowed from Moroccan chermoula, *which is used to flavor fish, meats, and poultry. Serve over cooked couscous or rice, with Celery and Lima Bean Puree (page 173), Sprouts and Sliced Tomato Salad (page 179), or Carrot Ribbons with Lemon and Cumin (page 180).*

serve 4 to 6

1 large onion, coarsely chopped

3 garlic cloves, thinly sliced

¼ cup olive oil

¼ teaspoon ground ginger

¼ teaspoon ground cinnamon

¼ teaspoon ground cumin

¼ teaspoon ground coriander

½ teaspoon hot red pepper flakes

½ cup raisins

1½ pounds cleaned squid

1½ cups chicken broth

One 15.5-ounce can chickpeas (garbanzos), rinsed and drained

2 tablespoons honey

2 tablespoons wine vinegar

1¼ cups sliced almonds

2 tablespoons butter

1 cup each roughly chopped fresh parsley and cilantro

1. In a large, heavy saucepan, cook the onion and garlic in the oil over moderate heat, stirring, until they begin to turn golden. Stir in the ginger, cinnamon, cumin, coriander, pepper flakes, and raisins, and cook for 1 minute. Add the squid and chicken broth and simmer, covered, for 25 minutes.

2. Stir in the chickpeas, honey, and vinegar and simmer, uncovered, for 10 minutes. Season with salt and pepper.

The stew can be made a day in advance. Let it cool, uncovered, before refrigerating it, covered.

3. In a medium skillet, cook the almonds in the butter, stirring over moderate heat until the nuts are golden. Transfer to a dish.

4. Serve the stew over couscous or rice topped with the almonds, parsley, and cilantro.

garlicky squid and artichokes with pasta shells

The slightly acidic flavor of the artichokes adds just the right balance to the buttery sauce. Eggless Caesar Salad (page 188) and good bread are all that is necessary to make a meal.

serves 4

1¼ pounds cleaned squid
   sacs and tentacles,
   defrosted if frozen

2 large garlic cloves, minced

½ stick (4 tablespoons) butter

2 tablespoons all-purpose
   flour

½ cup dry white wine

1 cup bottled clam juice

1 teaspoon dried thyme

¼ teaspoon pepper

One 14-ounce can artichoke
   hearts, drained and
   quartered

½ pound medium pasta
   shells

1. Cut the squid sacs into ½-inch rings and halve the tentacles.

2. In a large, deep skillet, cook the garlic in the butter over moderate heat, stirring, until pale golden. Add the flour and cook, stirring, for 1 minute. Add the wine, clam juice, thyme, and pepper, and simmer, stirring, for 2 minutes. Add the artichokes and simmer for 2 minutes.

The sauce can be made up to this point 8 hours in advance. Keep covered and chilled, and bring to a simmer before continuing.

3. Boil the pasta shells in a pot of boiling salted water until just tender. Drain but do not rinse.

4. Add the squid to the sauce and cook, stirring, until it turns white, about 2 minutes. Add the pasta and stir to coat with the sauce, adding a little water if necessary to thin. Serve immediately.

Note: By adding the squid at the last minute and only cooking it until opaque, it will be almost as tender as the pasta.

sausage-stuffed squid
in tomato and pepper sauce

This recipe takes some time, but it is not complicated. Squid sacs make perfect pouches for stuffing. They shrink considerably when cooked, keeping their contents snug inside; just make sure you leave enough space for the filling. Serve with cooked egg noodles or Baked Vegetable and Cheese Polenta (page 174) and Eggless Caesar Salad (page 188).

serves 4 to 6

2 pounds cleaned squid sacs, defrosted if frozen (see Notes)

½ pound sweet Italian sausage, casings removed (about 2½ links)

½ cup chopped onions

½ teaspoon dried thyme

1½ cups herb-seasoned stuffing mix

½ cup chopped fresh parsley

½ cup freshly grated Parmesan

1 large green bell pepper, seeded and sliced

¼ cup olive oil

2 garlic cloves, thinly sliced

Two 14.5-ounce cans diced tomatoes

2 teaspoons sugar

1. Remove the side flaps from the squid sacs and finely chop the flaps. Refrigerate the sacs until ready to stuff.

2. In a large, heavy skillet, cook the sausage, onion, and thyme over moderate heat, stirring and breaking up the meat, until it is cooked through. Add the chopped squid flaps and cook, stirring, for 2 minutes. Remove the skillet from the heat and stir in the stuffing mix, parsley, Parmesan, and black pepper to taste. Let cool.

3. In a large, deep skillet, cook the bell pepper in the oil over moderately high heat for 2 minutes. Add the garlic and cook, stirring, for 1 minute, or until it just begins to color. Add the tomatoes and sugar, and boil gently, stirring occasionally, for 10 minutes.

4. While the sauce is cooking, fill each squid sac loosely with the stuffing, leaving a 1-inch space at the opening, and press it closed (see Notes).

5. Add the sacs to the pan, shaking the pan to settle them in the sauce, and simmer, covered, for 30 to 40 minutes, or until the squid is tender. Serve as is or,

if preferred, slice each sac crosswise into rounds and top with the sauce.

Notes: Squid can be bought as frozen cleaned sacs only. If you can only find combined sacs and tentacles, 2 pounds yield about 1 pound of sacs. Reserve the tentacles for another recipe, or chop and add to the sauce.

Usually stuffed squid is secured with a toothpick at the end, but I find this an unnecessary and time-consuming step. Some of the stuffing may escape into the sauce, but this only enhances the sauce.

grilled squid with ginger garlic sauce

This steaklike squid is topped with an aromatic vinaigrette of scallions, garlic, and ginger. Serve with a hearty side dish, such as Orange Orzo with Basil (page 167) or Baked Vegetable and Cheese Polenta (page 174).

¼ cup soy sauce

3 tablespoons gin

2 tablespoons fresh lemon
  juice

2 teaspoons sugar

1½ pounds cleaned squid
  sacs, defrosted if frozen

2 tablespoons vegetable oil

1 cup chopped scallions
  (a.k.a. green onions)

1-inch piece fresh ginger,
  peeled and minced (about
  1½ tablespoons)

3 garlic cloves, minced (about
  1 tablespoon)

¼ cup seasoned rice vinegar

1. Stir together the soy sauce, gin, lemon juice, and sugar until the sugar is dissolved. Transfer to a sealable plastic bag, add the squid, and let marinate in the refrigerator for 2 to 8 hours.

2. In a small skillet, heat the oil over moderately high heat. Add the scallions and sauté, stirring, until beginning to brown, about 5 minutes. Add the ginger and garlic, and cook for 2 minutes. Remove the skillet from the heat and stir in the vinegar.

3. Drain the squid and grill on an oiled rack for about 2 minutes on each side until just cooked through. Transfer to a platter, top with the sauce, and sprinkle with pepper.

Note: The squid can also be served without the sauce. Just squeeze some lemon juice on top and sprinkle with pepper.

squid braised with lemon and olives

Serve this Mediterranean-style dish over plain rice or couscous, with Warm Herbed White Bean Salad (page 172) or Celery and Lima Bean Puree (page 173).

serves 4

1 onion, coarsely chopped

2 garlic cloves, minced

2 tablespoons olive oil

1 teaspoon ground cumin

¼ teaspoon ground
cinnamon

2 pounds cleaned squid sacs
and tentacles, defrosted if
frozen

¼ cup fresh lemon juice

4 slices lemon

½ cup bottled clam juice

½ cup small pimento-stuffed
olives

2 teaspoons cornstarch,
dissolved in 1 tablespoon
water

½ cup chopped fresh parsley

Cooked plain rice or
couscous

1. In a small flameproof casserole or small pot, cook the onion and garlic in the oil until they begin to turn golden. Add the cumin and cinnamon and cook, stirring, for 1 minute. Add the squid, lemon juice, lemon slices, clam juice, and olives, and simmer the mixture, covered, for 20 to 25 minutes, or until the squid is tender.

2. Stir in the cornstarch mixture and simmer for 1 minute. Stir in the parsley and season with salt and pepper. Serve over the rice or couscous.

Note: I prefer to leave the squid sacs and tentacles whole for this dish, as it seems more rustic somehow. Another option is to cut the sacs into rings and halve the tentacles.

Both of the following recipes start out identically. The addition of milk or chopped kale at the end distinguishes them completely.

new england–style squid chowder

Unlike clam chowder, you will not find this cream-based soup on every table in New England, but it is just as delicious. Serve with crusty bread or oyster crackers.

makes about 6 cups;
serves 4 to 6

8 ounces salt pork, cut into
¼-inch dice (about 1⅓
cups; see Note, page 156)

1 tablespoon olive oil

1 large onion, thinly sliced

2 large garlic cloves, minced

1 pound red potatoes (about
3 medium), peeled and cut
into ½-inch cubes

1½ pounds cleaned squid
sacs and tentacles,
coarsely chopped

1 cup chopped celery

3 cups bottled clam juice

1 teaspoon dried oregano

1 bay leaf

2 cups half-and-half

1. In a large, heavy pot, cook the salt pork in the oil over moderate heat, stirring occasionally, until browned, about 15 minutes. Add the onion and garlic and cook, stirring, until they begin to turn golden. Add the potatoes, squid, celery, clam juice, oregano, and bay leaf and simmer, partially covered, for 20 minutes.

2. Stir in the half-and-half and salt and pepper to taste, and heat the soup until very hot. Remove the bay leaf.

The soup can be made up to 1 day in advance, covered, and refrigerated.

squid, kale, and potato soup

Caldo verde *is a famous Portuguese soup, thickened with finely chopped greens and potatoes. Here, that classic is enhanced with tender squid and salt pork, resulting in a hearty, comforting main dish. Serve with good, crusty bread or Portuguese rolls, and Green Salad with Creamy Mustard Dressing and Sweet and Spicy Pecans (page 184).*

makes about 7 cups;
serves 4 to 6

8 ounces salt pork, cut into
   ¼-inch dice (about
   1⅓ cups; see Note)

1 tablespoon olive oil

1 large onion, thinly sliced

2 large garlic cloves, minced

1 pound red potatoes (about
   3 medium), peeled and cut
   into ½-inch cubes

1½ pounds cleaned squid
   sacs and tentacles,
   defrosted if frozen, coarsely
   chopped

3 to 4 cups bottled clam juice

1 teaspoon dried oregano

1 bay leaf

½ pound fresh kale

1 tablespoon wine vinegar

1. In a large, heavy pot, cook the salt pork in the oil over moderate heat, stirring occasionally, until browned, about 15 minutes. Add the onion and garlic and cook, stirring, until they begin to turn golden. Add the potatoes, squid, 3 cups of the clam juice, the oregano, and bay leaf and simmer, partially covered, for 20 minutes.

2. While the soup is simmering, rinse the kale and discard the tough center stems. In a food processor finely chop the kale. Stir into the soup with the vinegar and salt and pepper to taste. Simmer, uncovered, for 8 minutes. Add additional clam juice if the soup seems too thick. Remove the bay leaf.

Note: Salt pork is a cured bacon, and varies in its proportion of fat to meat. Some pieces (usually in prepackaged 8- to 12-ounce blocks) look like total fat, and some have more meat content. Either type adds a hearty but not overwhelming richness to the soup. Slab bacon can be substituted, but will add a smoky flavor.

mixed shellfish

A pristine boiled lobster, a bowl of glistening steamed mussels, or perfect pink shrimp sizzling in garlic butter are all treats in themselves, but combine these treasures from the sea in one dish and you have a truly spectacular feast. Shellfish have certain individual characteristics, but their flavors are similar enough to complement one another when combined.

All shellfish cooks quickly, so the trick to cooking more than one is timing. Sometimes the shellfish must be cooked individually before combining, or added in intervals so that everything finishes cooking at the same time.

Any of the recipes in this book can be adapted for mixed shellfish. Similar foods can be combined, such as clams and mussels. Add shrimp to Caramelized Peppered Scallops (page 63); add scallops to Crab Pasta Primavera (page 44); and add crab, shrimp, and/or scallops to Asian Lobster and Noodle Salad (page 129). Play around. Mix it up. But remember that live bivalves (clams, mussels, oysters, etc.) will add liquid to a dish, so plan accordingly.

chilled shellfish platter with chile vinaigrette and chive almond pesto

Simply poached pristine shellfish, showcased in this way, will certainly cause a buzz at any cocktail or dinner party. The two sauces add an exciting twist, but traditional lemon wedges and/or cocktail sauce can be included. Beautiful green-lipped New Zealand mussels and an assortment of different types of crab would really push it over the top. The shellfish can be cooked and chilled up to twelve hours in advance.

serves 4 as a main course
or 8 as hors d'oeuvres

8 large live mussels or frozen
on the half shell

8 sea scallops

8 large shrimp

2 Maine lobster tails or
4 small rock lobster tails,
halved lengthwise

½ to 1 pound jumbo lump
blue crabmeat, rinsed and
picked over for bits of
cartilage and shell, or
cocktail claws; or dungeness
crabmeat, cocktail claws,
or clusters; or snow crab
clusters; or king crab legs;
or stone crab claws

Chile Vinaigrette (recipe
follows)

Chive Almond Pesto (recipe
follows)

1. In a deep skillet, bring 2 cups water to a boil. Add the mussels and steam them, covered, 5 to 10 minutes, until the shells open (or until the mussels on the half shell are heated through). With a slotted spoon transfer the mussels to a plate, discarding the extra shells, and chill on the half shell, covered, until ready to serve.

2. Bring the liquid in the skillet to a boil, add the scallops, and cook for 1 minute. Add the shrimp and cook for 1 minute, or until the shellfish is just cooked through. With the slotted spoon transfer the shellfish to a plate and chill, covered, until ready to serve.

3. Bring the liquid in the skillet to a boil, add the lobster tails, cut side up, and steam them, covered, for 5 to 8 minutes, or until they are just cooked through. Transfer the lobster to a cutting board, remove the meat from each shell, and cut the meat crosswise into bite-size pieces. Return the meat to the shells and chill them, covered, until ready to serve.

4. Arrange the shellfish, including the crabmeat, decoratively on a large platter or tiered tray. Serve with the sauces and small cocktail forks.

chile vinaigrette

½ cup vegetable oil

¼ cup chopped shallots

1 tablespoon chile powder

⅓ cup fresh lime or lemon
   juice

2 teaspoons sugar

½ teaspoon salt

¼ teaspoon freshly ground
   black pepper

makes about 1 cup

In a small skillet, heat ¼ cup of the oil, the shallot, and chile powder over moderate heat until the mixture sizzles. Let it sizzle, stirring for 1 minute, and transfer to a blender. Add the remaining ¼ cup oil, the lime juice, sugar, salt, and pepper and blend the vinaigrette until smooth.

The vinaigrette keeps, covered and chilled, for up to 1 week.

chive almond pesto

⅓ cup whole natural almonds

1 cup chopped fresh chives

½ cup olive oil

1 small garlic clove, chopped

¼ cup water

1 tablespoon fresh lime or
   lemon juice

1 teaspoon salt

½ teaspoon freshly ground
   black pepper

makes about 1 cup

In a blender, grind the almonds fine. Add the chives and blend until pureed. Scrape the sides and bottom of the beaker, add the remaining ingredients, and blend the pesto until smooth.

The pesto keeps, covered and chilled, for up to 1 week.

truly simple bouillabaisse

Today bouillabaisse is thought of as an extravagant, white-tablecloth type of dish, but it was origi-nally created by fishermen as a simple way to prepare whatever fish and shellfish were around. In the spirit of its origins, I offer this modern version of the famous soup. Purists may gasp, but surely if the hardworking fishermen of long ago had had conveniences like preseasoned canned tomatoes and bot-tled clam juice, they would have used them to simplify their cooking. Feel free to add different fish and shellfish; just don't overcook it. On the side, try serving Orange Orzo with Basil (page 167), Warm Herbed White Bean Salad (page 172), or Eggless Caesar Salad (page 188).

serves 4

1 large onion, coarsely
  chopped

3 tablespoons olive oil

One 14.5-ounce can chopped
  tomatoes with jalapeños,
  including juice

2 cups bottled clam juice or
  shellfish stock (see
  page 4)

1 teaspoon dried thyme

for the toasts

4 thick slices French bread

1 peeled garlic clove

8 teaspoons mayonnaise

16 to 20 mussels, scrubbed
  well

16 small hard-shell clams,
  scrubbed well

1. In a large, heavy-bottomed pot, cook the onion in the oil over moderate heat, stirring, until it begins to brown, about 15 minutes. Add the tomatoes, clam juice, and thyme and simmer, uncovered, for 15 minutes.

The soup can be prepared up to this point 2 hours in advance.

2. Toast the bread slices until very crisp. Rub each toast generously with the garlic clove and spread each with 2 teaspoons mayonnaise.

3. When ready to serve, bring the tomato broth to a boil. Add the mussels and clams and cook, covered, for 2 minutes, shaking the pan. Immediately add the shrimp and scallops and cook, covered, for 3 minutes. Finally add the squid, stir the soup gently and cook, covered, 1 minute more.

½ pound peeled shrimp

½ pound sea scallops

½ pound squid, sacs cut into rings and tentacles halved if large

4. Remove the pot from the heat. Put a prepared toast in each of four shallow soup dishes. Ladle the shellfish and broth on top and serve immediately.

Note: Rubbing the toasts with garlic provides the soup with its characteristic hearty flavor. This is a quick way to replace the traditional rouille, *or garlic-flavored mayonnaise.*

scallop, shrimp, and crab salad with tarragon mayonnaise

Any combination of your favorite shellfish can be used in this salad, which is perfect for warm-weather entertaining. Serve it with Quick Pickled Green Beans (page 178), Sprouts and Sliced Tomato Salad (page 179), or Carrot Ribbons with Lemon and Cumin (page 180).

serves 4

¼ cup dry white wine or vermouth

2 sprigs fresh tarragon, plus 1 tablespoon chopped tarragon leaves

1 bay leaf

¼ teaspoon salt

¼ teaspoon freshly ground black pepper

½ pound sea scallops, rinsed and halved horizontally, or bay scallops

½ pound shrimp, peeled and deveined

¼ cup minced shallots

½ cup mayonnaise

1 tablespoon fresh lemon juice

½ pound fine-quality crabmeat, checked for pieces of cartilage

1 small red or orange bell pepper, diced

½ cup very thinly sliced celery

1. In a large saucepan, bring 1 cup water and the wine to a boil with the tarragon sprigs, bay leaf, salt, and pepper. Add the scallops and shrimp and cook, stirring, for 1 to 2 minutes, or until the fish is just cooked through. With a slotted spoon, transfer the shellfish to a large bowl, leaving the herbs in the pan, and cover and refrigerate until cold, about 1 hour.

2. Add the shallot to the pan and boil until the liquid is reduced to about 3 tablespoons. Transfer to a large bowl, discarding the tarragon sprigs and bay leaf, and let cool.

3. In the large bowl, whisk together the reduced stock, mayonnaise, and lemon juice. Add the chilled shellfish, crabmeat, bell pepper, celery, chopped tarragon, and salt and pepper to taste, and toss well.

chesapeake chowder with smoked sausage

*T*his soup is based on one that I had at a small restaurant, set on the edge of the Chesapeake Bay. It is a reminder of how incredible the Chesapeake Bay's resources are, and how important it is to preserve the health of the United States' largest estuary. Make this the center of a meal, served with good bread, Sprouts and Sliced Tomato Salad (page 179), Red, White, and Blue Slaw (page 183), or Eggless Caesar Salad (page 188).

makes 8 cups; serves 4 as a main course

4 ounces smoked sausage, such as kielbasa, cut into ¼-inch dice (1 cup)

1 medium onion, chopped (about 1½ cups)

1 tablespoon olive oil

2 medium boiling potatoes, peeled and cut into ½-inch pieces (about 2 cups)

12 small hard-shell clams, scrubbed

2 cups bottled clam juice

1 teaspoon dried thyme

1 cup frozen or fresh corn kernels

1 cup heavy cream

2 tablespoons all-purpose flour

1 pint shucked oysters (about 2 dozen), including their liquor, if necessary

½ pound fine-quality crabmeat

1. In a large, heavy saucepan, cook the sausage and onion in the oil over moderate heat, stirring, until they begin to turn golden, about 15 minutes. Add the potatoes, clams, clam juice, and thyme and boil, covered, for 2 to 5 minutes, transferring the clams as they open to a bowl. Add the corn and simmer for 2 minutes more, or until the potatoes are just tender.

2. In a small bowl, stir together the cream and flour until smooth. Whisk into the saucepan and simmer, stirring, for 2 minutes.

3. Add the oysters and heat until their edges begin to curl.

4. Add the cooked clams, crabmeat, and salt and pepper to taste, and bring the chowder to a simmer. Serve immediately.

shellfish lasagna

Even though this recipe has many steps, it is easy to prepare and can be made a day in advance. Serve with a good bread, or garlic bread, and Green Salad with Creamy Mustard Dressing and Sweet and Spicy Pecans (page 184), Green Salad with Grapes and Sunflower Seeds (page 187), or Eggless Caesar Salad (page 188).

serves 6 to 8

1 pound peeled shrimp

1 pound sea or bay scallops

1 pound trimmed fresh or
   frozen spinach

1 medium onion, coarsely
   chopped (about 1½ cups)

2 cups coarsely chopped
   fennel bulb (1 small bulb) or
   celery

2 tablespoons olive oil

1 teaspoon dried thyme

1 teaspoon dried tarragon

½ cup dry white wine

2 cups chopped tomatoes
   (2 medium tomatoes)

½ pound fine-quality
   crabmeat, checked for
   pieces of cartilage

6 (4 X 7-inch) "no-boil" or
   "oven-ready" lasagna
   noodles (see Note)

1. Halve the shrimp lengthwise and if using sea scallops, halve them horizontally into thinner rounds.

2. Bring 4 inches of salted water to a boil in a large pot and add the spinach. Cook, stirring, for 2 minutes and drain in a colander. Let the spinach drain and cool. Squeeze it dry and chop it coarsely.

3. In a large, deep skillet, cook the onion and fennel in the oil over moderate heat, stirring, until softened, 5 to 8 minutes. Add the thyme, tarragon, wine, and tomatoes, and bring to a boil. Add the scallops and shrimp and cook, stirring, for 3 to 5 minutes, or until barely cooked through. Stir in the crabmeat and immediately transfer the mixture to a sieve set over a bowl and let drain.

4. Soak the pasta noodles in a dish of hot water for 10 minutes. Drain and reserve on paper towels. In a bowl toss together the cheeses and reserve.

5. Make the béchamel: Pour the strained seafood juices into a large measuring cup (one that holds at least 3 cups). Add enough milk to the cup to measure 2½ cups.

¼ pound shredded Gruyère
or Jarlsberg (about
1½ cups)
½ pound shredded
mozzarella (about 2 cups)

for the béchamel
sauce

1 to 2 cups milk
½ stick (4 tablespoons) butter
½ cup flour

In the large, deep skillet, melt the butter over moderately low heat. Stir in the flour and cook the roux, stirring, for 1 minute. Whisk in the milk mixture, bring to a boil, whisking constantly, and simmer for 3 minutes. Stir in the shellfish and vegetables, and add salt and pepper to taste.

6. Preheat the oven to 400°F.

7. Lay 2 soaked lasagna noodles in the bottom of a 9-inch square baking pan. Top with one-half of the shellfish mixture, one-half of the spinach, and one-third of the cheese. Cover with another layer of lasagna noodles, the remaining shellfish and spinach, and one-half of the remaining cheese. End with a layer of noodles topped with the remaining cheese. The lasagna can be baked immediately or covered and chilled for up to 24 hours.

8. Bake the lasagna, uncovered, for about 40 minutes if baking immediately, for 1 hour if chilled, or until a metal knife inserted in the center comes out hot.

Note: If preferred, regular boiled lasagna noodles can be used, cooked according to package directions.

orange orzo with basil

Boiling pasta in orange juice leaves it with a sweet flavor and golden color. Experiment with different pastas and herbs such as thyme, rosemary, and sage for a new twist.

serves 4 to 6

4 cups orange juice

1 tablespoon vegetable oil

1 teaspoon salt

½ pound orzo (rice-shaped pasta)

4 tablespoons butter

¼ cup chopped fresh basil

2 tablespoons freshly grated Parmesan

1. In a large saucepan, bring the orange juice, 1 cup water, the oil, and salt to a boil. Add the orzo and boil, stirring often until just tender, about 10 minutes. Drain in a sieve and rinse.

2. Return the orzo to the pan, add the butter, and heat over moderate heat, stirring until the butter is melted. Stir in the basil, Parmesan, and salt and pepper to taste.

jollof rice

There is no single correct recipe for Jollof rice, which is popular among countries on the west coast of Africa, and ranges from a paella-type casserole to a plain rice side dish. I am most familiar with the version that our church members from Nigeria and Sierra Leone bring to potluck dinners. Jollof rice always accompanies a saucy dish of stewed fish, goat, or chicken in order to soak up the flavorful juices. Think pilaf and you'll understand this dish.

serves 6

1 medium onion, chopped (about 1½ cups)

2 tablespoons vegetable or olive oil

1 large tomato, chopped (about 1¼ cups)

1 teaspoon sweet paprika

¼ teaspoon cayenne pepper or hot red pepper flakes

1½ cups long-grain white rice

1½ cups chicken broth

½ teaspoon salt

1 carrot, peeled and finely chopped (about ¾ cup)

1 cup frozen peas

1. In a large, heavy saucepan, with a tight-fitting lid, cook the onion in the oil over moderate heat, stirring until softened.

2. Add the tomato, paprika, and cayenne, and simmer, stirring, 1 minute. Stir in the rice, coating it well with the juices, and stir in the broth and salt.

3. Simmer the rice, covered, for 15 minutes. Stir in the carrot and peas and cook the rice, covered, over low heat for 10 minutes more, or until the rice is tender.

potato salad with roasted peppers and sesame seeds

This potato salad is a refreshing alternative to the classic creamy style. It is suitable for a picnic, but also works as a side dish for a more formal meal.

2½ to 3 pounds boiling
potatoes (see Notes)

⅓ cup seasoned rice vinegar

¼ cup vegetable oil

1 teaspoon salt

One 7-ounce jar roasted red
peppers, drained and
chopped

1 cup chopped celery

½ cup thinly sliced scallions
(a.k.a. green onions)

Freshly ground black pepper
to taste

1 tablespoon toasted sesame
seeds

1. In a large pot, cover the potatoes with water. Bring the water to a boil, reduce to a simmer, and cook 10 to 20 minutes, or until the potatoes are just tender when tested with the tip of a knife. Immediately drain and rinse with cold water to stop the cooking.

2. Peel the potatoes and cut into bite-size pieces (see Notes). Add the vinegar, oil, and salt, and toss well. Add the remaining ingredients and toss well. The salad can be served at room temperature or chilled.

Notes: The cooking time for the potatoes depends on their size. Large boiling potatoes work as well as small ones. Test with the tip of a sharp knife or long bamboo skewer. It should easily penetrate the potato to its center.

To peel the hot potato, hold it on a fork and, with your other hand, peel it with a paring knife.

two potato hash

Rather than keeping the potatoes in a pancake shape, they can also be turned by sections. Continue to cook and turn the mixture until it is as browned and crisped as desired.

serves 4

¾- to 1-pound all-purpose
   potato, peeled and
   shredded
¾- to 1-pound sweet potato,
   peeled and shredded
2 tablespoons olive oil
2 tablespoons butter

1. In a large bowl, toss together the shredded potatoes.

2. In a large nonstick skillet (10 inches or larger), heat the oil and butter over moderate heat until bubbling. Add the potatoes and pat into the pan evenly. Cover and cook for 8 to 10 minutes, or until the underside is golden.

3. Invert a baking sheet over the skillet and flip the potato pancake onto the sheet. Slide the pancake into the skillet and cook, uncovered, another 5 to 8 minutes, or until golden and crisp on the bottom. Sprinkle with salt and pepper to taste, cut into wedges, and serve.

The hash can be made up to 1 hour in advance and reheated gently in the skillet.

grapefruit rice with chives

This rice, which picks up a subtle light flavor from the grapefruit juice, goes well with any seafood dish. If chive flowers are available, pull them apart and sprinkle them on top for an added beautiful lilac color and spicy flavor.

serves 4

2 tablespoons olive oil

1¼ cups long-grain rice

1½ cups fresh grapefruit
   juice

¾ teaspoon salt

½ cup chopped chives or
   scallion greens (a.k.a. green
   onions)

1. In a large, heavy saucepan, heat the oil over moderately high heat. Add the rice and cook, stirring, for 2 minutes, or until the rice begins to turn a chalky white.

2. Add ½ cup water, the grapefruit juice, and salt, and bring to a boil. Boil the rice uncovered, without stirring, until the liquid has evaporated and holes appear on the surface of the rice.

3. Cover the saucepan and immediately reduce the heat to low. Let the rice cook for 20 minutes, or until tender. Stir in the chives and salt and pepper to taste.

Note: Cooking rice by quickly boiling off the excess water and steaming until done is a technique I learned from a Cuban friend. Having control over how fast the liquid evaporates helps to prevent overcooked, mushy rice. When I don't use my rice cooker, this is the way I cook all my rice.

warm herbed white bean salad

Canned beans are a super convenient food, offering good taste and a wide range of nutritional benefits as well. Fresh fennel (often mislabled as anise) can be substituted for the celery, giving the dish a faint licorice flavor.

serves 4

One 15- to 16-ounce can
small white beans

½ cup chopped celery (about
2 ribs)

¼ cup olive oil

2 large garlic cloves, minced

1½ tablespoons wine vinegar

¼ cup chopped fresh parsley

1 teaspoon chopped fresh
thyme or ¼ teaspoon
dried thyme

Freshly ground black pepper

1. In a sieve, rinse and drain the beans well.

2. In a medium skillet, cook the celery in the oil over moderate heat for 2 minutes. Add the garlic and cook, stirring, until the garlic begins to color, about 1 minute. Add the beans and cook until they are just heated through, and remove the skillet from the heat.

3. Stir in the vinegar, parsley, thyme, and pepper to taste. Serve warm.

celery and lima bean puree

The starch in lima beans gives this puree the texture of mashed potatoes, but its pale green color and fresh taste are not as heavy.

2 garlic cloves, minced

3 tablespoons olive oil

2 cups chopped celery,
including any leaves

1 pound (about 3 cups) frozen
lima beans

1. In a large, heavy saucepan, cook the garlic in the oil over moderate heat, stirring, for 2 minutes. Add ½ cup water and the celery and simmer, covered, for 4 minutes. Add the lima beans and simmer, covered, for 10 minutes, or until the beans are tender.

2. Puree the mixture in a food processor until smooth, adding salt and pepper to taste.

The puree can be made 1 day in advance. Reheat in the microwave or in a pot over low heat on the stove, stirring often, or covered in a 300°F oven.

baked vegetable and cheese polenta

This polenta makes a delicious accompaniment to sautéed, grilled, or stewed shellfish. It also makes a satisfying brunch dish and can be served with everything from eggs to roast beef.

serves 8

One 14½-ounce can chicken broth

¾ cup thinly sliced scallions (a.k.a. green onions)

1 cup fresh or frozen corn kernels (1 ear of corn)

½ teaspoon dried thyme

1¾ cups yellow cornmeal

2 teaspoons salt

½ teaspoon black pepper

2 tomatoes, seeded and chopped (about 2 cups)

1 medium zucchini, scrubbed and diced

8 ounces mozzarella, cut into ¼-inch dice

½ cup chopped fresh basil

2 tablespoons butter

1. Butter a 9-inch square baking dish. Preheat the oven to 350°F.

2. Bring the broth, scallions, corn, and thyme to a boil in a large, heavy saucepan. In a large bowl stir together the cornmeal and 4¼ cups water, and add to the broth, stirring. Simmer the polenta, stirring, for 10 minutes and add the salt and pepper.

3. Remove from the heat and stir in the tomatoes and zucchini. Add the mozzarella and basil, stirring just to combine, and pour into the baking dish. Dot the top with the butter.

The polenta can be made 1 day in advance, covered, and chilled.

4. Bake, covered, for 45 minutes. Uncover and bake 30 minutes more, or until golden.

Note: Stirring the cornmeal with water before adding the hot liquid keeps the polenta from getting lumpy.

summer corn on the cob with basil butter

It is hard to improve on perfect summer corn on the cob with butter, but fresh basil adds a special twist and a complementary flavor of the sun.

serves 6 to 12

1 dozen ears fresh corn, shucked

1 cup fresh basil leaves

6 tablespoons butter

1. Put the corn in a large pot and cover with cold water. Bring the water to a boil and immediately remove from the heat. The corn is ready to eat in 10 minutes, but can be kept warm in the water for 30 minutes.

2. In a food processor or blender, puree the basil. Melt the butter and add to the basil with salt and pepper to taste. Puree the mixture until smooth.

3. Drain the corn and serve with the basil butter.

sliced asparagus and edamame with olive oil

Green on green and refreshing with any main course, this simple, healthy side dish should become a regular on your table. Frozen soybeans have become so popular, they are available nearly everywhere, snuggled between the frozen peas and corn.

serves 4 to 6

6 ounces (1½ cups) frozen
    shelled edamame (fresh
    soybeans)
½ pound fresh asparagus,
    rinsed, trimmed, and cut
    into 1-inch pieces
1½ tablespoons extra virgin
    olive oil

1. In a saucepan of salted boiling water, cook the edamame for 4 minutes. Add the asparagus and boil for 2 to 3 minutes more, or until the asparagus is tender but still crisp. Drain in a colander and rinse briefly under cold water.

2. Return the vegetables to the saucepan, add the oil and salt and pepper to taste. Keep warm until ready to serve.

variations

Melt some butter with lime, lemon, or orange juice in
    place of the olive oil.
Stir in scallions, chives, fresh tarragon, basil, or parsley.
Sauté a minced garlic clove in the oil before adding the
    vegetables.

roasted maple butter acorn squash

Winter squash may not seem like an obvious accompaniment for seafood, but its light nutty flavor is delicious with the rich, briny flavors of the ocean.

serves 4 to 8

2 small acorn squashes

2 tablespoons butter, cut into
   8 pieces

2 tablespoons maple syrup

1. Preheat the oven to 375°F.

2. Cut each squash into 4 wedges and scrape out the seeds and strings. Arrange in a single layer, skin sides down, in a baking dish. Top each wedge with a piece of butter and drizzle with maple syrup.

3. Cover with aluminum foil and bake 30 minutes. Uncover and bake another 30 minutes. Season with salt and pepper.

quick pickled green beans

These quickly pickled beans are a refreshing side dish, or they can be chilled and served with cheese as an hors d'oeuvre.

serves 4

1 pound green string beans,
    trimmed

½ cup white wine vinegar

½ cup seasoned rice vinegar

3 garlic cloves, thinly sliced

2 tablespoons sugar

2 tablespoons salt

1 teaspoon hot red pepper
    flakes, or to taste

1. In a pot of boiling salted water, cook the beans for 3 to 5 minutes, or until tender but crisp. Drain and rinse briefly under cold water.

2. In a heavy sealable plastic bag, mix together the remaining ingredients. Add the warm beans, seal the bag, and turn to mix well. The beans are ready to eat warm or at room temperature in 10 minutes. Or keep, chilled, for up to 1 week.

sprouts and sliced tomato salad

There are many sprouts to choose from in today's market—radish, broccoli, and spicy are next to the old familiars, alfalfa and mung bean. Whether it's a mixture or an old favorite, you will love them piled high on beautiful sliced tomatoes, accented with fresh herbs and lightly seasoned.

serves 4 to 6

3 tomatoes, cored and sliced

One container of sprouts,
   such as alfalfa, radish,
   onion, or a mixture

¼ cup chopped fresh
   cilantro, basil, and/or mint

1 tablespoon lime juice

2 tablespoons olive oil

Arrange the tomato slices so that they are overlapping in a circle on a platter. Scatter the sprouts on top with the herbs. Drizzle the salad with the lime juice and oil, and sprinkle with salt and pepper.

carrot ribbons with lemon and cumin

Cutting carrots into thin bands is a different and dramatic way to serve them. Cumin and lemon make them especially appealing with spicy or rich dishes. It is a tasty side dish for seafood, but is equally delicious with poultry, pork, and lamb.

serves 4

¾ pound carrots

⅓ cup extra virgin olive oil

2 tablespoons fresh lemon
   juice

½ teaspoon ground cumin

Peel the carrots and, with a vegetable peeler, shred the carrots lengthwise into "ribbons." In a medium bowl toss them with the oil, lemon juice, cumin, and salt and pepper to taste.

mom's coleslaw

My mother is always asked to bring her coleslaw to summer events. It is so simple but perfectly balanced.

makes 8 cups; serves 6

1 small head green cabbage

1 cup mayonnaise

1 tablespoon grated onions

1 tablespoon wine vinegar

1 tablespoon sugar

1 tablespoon Dijon mustard

1. Quarter the cabbage and cut out the tough core. Slice the cabbage with a sharp knife into shreds and add to a large bowl (there should be about 8 cups).

2. In a small bowl, whisk together the mayonnaise, onion, vinegar, sugar, mustard, and salt and pepper to taste. Add to the cabbage and toss well.

carolina vinegar slaw

This slaw is a great alternative to a mayonnaise-based one. It is perfect for cutting the richness of Carolina pork barbecue, and pairs equally well with full-flavored shellfish. It will seem like a lot of cabbage, but it shrinks after standing awhile.

1 small head cabbage,
   shredded (8 to 10 cups)

1 green bell pepper, thinly
   sliced

1 red bell pepper, thinly sliced

1 medium onion, thinly sliced

1¼ cups cider vinegar

¾ cup sugar

1 teaspoon salt

1 teaspoon celery seeds

1 teaspoon dry mustard

½ cup vegetable oil

1. In a large bowl, toss together the cabbage, bell peppers, and onion.

2. In a medium saucepan, bring the vinegar to a boil with the sugar, salt, celery seeds, and mustard, stirring to dissolve the sugar. Pour the hot liquid over the cabbage with the oil and toss well. Let the slaw sit for 15 to 30 minutes, tossing occasionally, and season with salt and pepper.

red, white, and blue slaw

This is an obvious choice for a Fourth of July cookout. The red cabbage actually looks more blue than red. It also pairs well with shellfish and fish when a light, vinaigrette-based slaw is desired.

serves 6 to 8

½ cup rice vinegar

½ cup vegetable oil

2 tablespoons Dijon mustard

2 teaspoons sugar

4 cups finely shredded red
cabbage

4 cups finely shredded white
cabbage

2 red bell peppers, cut into
thin slivers

½ cup toasted slivered
almonds

In a large bowl, whisk together the vinegar, oil, mustard, and sugar. Just before serving add the cabbages, bell peppers, and almonds and toss well. Season with salt and pepper to taste.

green salad with creamy mustard dressing and sweet and spicy pecans

This salad combines many of the great flavors of New Orleans. The tangy mustard dressing is balanced with crisp pecans that have both the sweetness of pralines and the fire of cayenne pepper.

serves 4

1 tablespoon Dijon mustard

2 teaspoons mayonnaise

1 tablespoon fresh lemon
   juice

1 teaspoon freshly grated
   onions

⅓ cup olive oil

5 cups torn Boston and/or
   romaine lettuce leaves

1 cup watercress sprigs,
   coarse stems discarded

Sweet and Spicy Pecans
   (recipe follows)

1. Whisk together the mustard, mayonnaise, lemon juice, and onion until smooth. Whisk in the oil in a stream and add salt and pepper to taste.

2. In a large salad bowl, toss the lettuce and watercress with the dressing. Serve the salad on plates and sprinkle each serving with some of the nuts.

sweet and spicy pecans

2 cups pecan halves

1 tablespoon butter

½ cup firmly packed brown
   sugar

½ teaspoon salt

⅛ to ¼ teaspoon cayenne
   pepper

1. In a large nonstick skillet, cook the pecans in the butter over moderate heat until they are hot, about 3 minutes. Add the brown sugar. Cook the nuts, stirring constantly over moderate to moderately high heat, for 3 to 5 minutes, or until the sugar is no longer granular and is clinging to the nuts. (If it appears that the sugar is burning, reduce the heat.)

2. Remove the skillet from the heat and sprinkle the salt and cayenne to taste evenly over the nuts. Stir to combine well and let the nuts cool.

The nuts can be kept in an airtight container for up to 2 weeks.

Note: The nuts alone make a great hors d'oeuvre or gift.

spinach salad with blue cheese and plum dressing

Because this salad has the assertive flavors of blue cheese and a fruity dressing, it pairs best with dishes with less complex flavors such as Shrimp and Sausage Kebabs (page 16) or plain poached seafood.

serves 4

5 cups fresh baby spinach
leaves, washed and
spun dry

1 ripe plum

⅓ cup vegetable oil

3 tablespoons red wine
vinegar

¼ cup crumbled blue or goat
cheese

1. Put the spinach in a salad bowl.

2. Wash and pit the plum. Put it in a blender and add the oil and vinegar. Blend the dressing until smooth and season with salt and pepper to taste.

3. Sprinkle the spinach with the cheese and drizzle with the dressing to taste.

Leftover dressing can be kept, covered and refrigerated, for 1 week.

green salad with grapes and sunflower seeds

Whole parsley leaves in a salad add a distinct, fresh herby taste, which stands up to the sweet grapes and salty sunflower seeds.

serves 6

3 tablespoons red wine
   vinegar

1/2 teaspoon salt

1/4 teaspoon black pepper

2 teaspoons Dijon mustard

Pinch of sugar

1/3 cup olive oil

8 cups torn mixed lettuce

1 cup flat-leaf (or Italian)
   parsley, rinsed and spun
   dry

1 1/2 cups red seedless
   grapes, halved

1/4 cup shelled, roasted
   sunflower seeds

1. In a small bowl, whisk together the vinegar, salt, pepper, mustard, and sugar. Add the oil and whisk until emulsified.

2. In a large salad bowl, combine the lettuce, parsley, and grapes, and toss with the dressing. Sprinkle with the sunflower seeds and serve immediately.

eggless caesar salad

The mayonnaise in this dressing replaces the creaminess of a raw egg yolk, and the anchovy paste adds a meaty saltiness. The time-consuming part of this recipe is making the croutons, but the home-made kind are so much better than store-bought, it's worth the effort.

serves 6 to 8

for the croutons

¼ cup olive oil

4 cups 1-inch bread cubes, cut from an Italian or French baguette

1 large garlic clove

½ teaspoon salt

¼ cup fresh lemon juice

1 teaspoon Worcestershire sauce

2 teaspoons Dijon mustard

2 tablespoons mayonnaise

1 teaspoon anchovy paste

¾ cup olive oil

1 large head romaine, torn, rinsed, and spun dry

½ cup freshly grated Parmesan

1. Make the croutons: In a large skillet, heat the oil over moderate heat and add the bread cubes. Toast them, turning constantly until they are golden, and transfer to a plate. Sprinkle them with salt and pepper to taste.

2. On a cutting board, mash the garlic and salt with a fork until it forms a paste, and transfer it to a salad bowl. Add the lemon juice, Worcestershire sauce, mustard, mayonnaise, and anchovy paste, and whisk until smooth. Add the oil in a stream, whisking constantly until the dressing is emulsified, and season with salt and pepper.

The dressing keeps, covered and chilled, for up to 4 days.

3. Add the lettuce and toss to coat the leaves. Add the Parmesan and croutons, and toss well. Serve immediately.